Unmaking Goliath

Unmaking Goliath

*Community Control
in the Face of Global Capital*

by James DeFilippis

ROUTLEDGE
NEW YORK AND LONDON

Published in 2004 by
Routledge
29 West 35th Street
New York, NY 10001
www.routledge-ny.com

Published in Great Britain by
Routledge
11 New Fetter Lane
London EC4P 4EE
www.routledge.co.uk

Routledge is an imprint of the Taylor and Francis Group.

Printed in the United Stated of America on acid-free paper.

10 9 8 7 6 5 4 3 2 1

Library of Congress Cataloging-in-Publication Data

DeFilippis, James.
  Unmaking Goliath : community control in the face of global capital /
by James DeFilippis.
      p. cm.
Includes bibliographical references and index.
  ISBN 0-415-94524-0 (alk. paper) — ISBN 0-415-94525-9 (pbk. : alk. paper)
 1. Government ownership—United States. 2. Municipal ownership—United States. 3. Collectivism—United States. 4. Local government—United States. 5. Globalization. I. Title.
  HD3885D44 2003
  330.12'6—dc21
                                                                    2003010246

Contents

Acknowledgments

This book benefited greatly from the encouragement, criticism, and support of many of those around me. It originated as a Ph.D. thesis at Rutgers, and has accompanied me wherever I've gone in the years since then. I have been very fortunate to be in extremely supportive environments as I've worked on this book—as a Ph.D. student at Rutgers; as a lecturer at King's College London; Housing Policy Analyst at the Community Service Society; and finally in the Department of Black and Hispanic Studies at Baruch College—at the sites where I conducted my fieldwork and, most importantly, at home.

I have often thought that when you're a graduate student you learn as much from your classmates as you do from the faculty members with whom you work, and that was certainly my experience at Rutgers. I learned and benefited from many of the graduate students I was lucky enough to be surrounded by. And while there were too many supportive friends and colleagues at Rutgers to name them all, in particular, Joe Center, Laura Liu, and Melina Patterson, all gave me more ideas, challenges, friendship, and support than they will probably ever know. The important role of graduate students notwithstanding, I learned a great deal from the faculty I was fortunate enough to work with at Rutgers. Elvin Wyly is a great colleague and friend who forced me to broaden my frame of reference to include many works, especially on issues of housing and labor markets, that I would otherwise not have encountered. Susan Fainstein, who almost scared me out of graduate school in my first semester, has been a powerful intellectual figure for me. She forced me to examine works I agree with just as critically as I would those that I don't, insured that I keep my mind open to arguments I would not have otherwise taken seriously, and made sure I didn't slip too much into the disciplinary limits of geography. Neil Smith was someone I worked very closely with in my time at Rutgers, and I am extremely grateful for the political and intellectual guidance and support he provided. Finally, Bob Lake was the most supportive and encouraging mentor, advisor, editor, copresenter, coauthor, boss, and friend I could have wanted. He has made my work much better, and this book is in no small part just as much his as it is mine. I am therefore more grateful to him than anyone else I've worked with on this book.

The dissertation became a book (at least as an idea) when I was a lecturer at King's College, London. While I was only at King's for two and a half years, it was a very supportive environment, and in many ways wish I could have stayed longer. My colleagues at King's were great, and the "Cities Research Group" of Iain Black, David Green, Chris Hamnett, Keith Hoggart, Loretta Lees, and, particularly, Margaret Byron, was an excellent group of people with whom to work. Everyone should be lucky enough to have such a group to work with in their first academic job. I also worked closely with people in London outside King's who were very helpful in my attempts to understand and participate in urban politics there. Most significant was Pete North, who deserves an acknowledgment here. In my time at CSS, I was intellectually and politically re-energized, being back home fighting for basic issues of justice and equity in New York. Victor Bach, in particular, was a very productive and encouraging person to work with. Finally, my time at Baruch has only recently begun, but I am excited about the new avenues of research and teaching that will come in my time. And the staff has been very supportive of me and my work.

Part of the requirements and joys of doing "action research" is that you work with groups that you believe in, and that believe in you enough to give you their time and energy as you work. Any criticism of these groups in this book is made from the perspective of an unapologetic supporter of them, their work, and their accomplishments. I was very lucky that the case-study sites where I worked allowed me this opportunity. I hope that my interaction with them has been useful in some way. In particular, the staffs and boards of Bethex Federal Credit Union and the Mutual Housing Association of Southwestern Connecticut were very generous with their very limited time. The Industrial Cooperatives of America (the ICA Group) was similarly supportive, as were those involved in the buyout at Marland Mold. I also benefited from countless conversations with community development practitioners, funders, and researchers—and there are too many to list—whose ideas and input were greatly appreciated and played a huge role in the completion of this work. Finally, the workers, residents, and members of the collectives I've worked with, and other people in these localities took so much of their time to talk with me, respond to surveys and, ultimately, make this book possible.

Lastly, my friends and family have always been supportive of me. My family has always created an environment where questions of equity and justice not only *could* be asked in our daily lives, but really *should* be asked—political discussions dominate our family gatherings. So in many ways, this book could not have been conceived or completed without them. My parents, Daisy and Nunzio (and Daisy even gave the book its title . . .), and my siblings, David, Nicky, Nunzio, and Christie, have all provided me with an eternal source of love and support (and Nicky even read and commented with his critical-thinking activist's eye on a complete draft of this book). Whatever I fail at, it is not, and never has been, for lack of a supportive family. Allison's family, Norma, Marv, Steve, and Lesley, have also always been very supportive of me and my work, and that has made this work much easier. Lastly there's Allison, who has had to put up with so much over the years that this book has been in the making. There are very few people in the world who would be as tirelessly generous, enthusiastic, supportive, and willing to listen to me think out loud about work in the supermarket (or on the subway, in the car, or sitting up late at night, or walking down the street . . .). I am incredibly grateful for all that she's done for me, and, therefore, this book is dedicated to her.

Introduction

All politics is local, it is often said. But what about economics? Politics in this country,
Americans like to believe, are participatory and democratic. But what about economics?
—*Berkshire Eagle*, 1992

Anybody who makes a prediction has in fact a "programme" for whose victory he is
working, and his prediction is precisely an element contributing to that victory . . .
Indeed one might say that only to the extent to which the objective aspect of
prediction is linked to a programme does it acquire its objectivity.
—Antonio Gramsci, *The Modern Prince*

I begin this book with the two quotes above because they exemplify the
two sets of issues and questions that form its very core. The first quote
comes from the local newspaper as the city of Pittsfield, Massachusetts,
struggled to keep a modestly profitable plant open after its multinational
corporate owner decided to close it and relocate production to a nonunion
shop in Florida. I begin with this, because it is *exactly* this reality: one of
consistently increasing levels of alienation from the structures that govern
our lives, and declining standards of living—even in times and places experiencing aggregate levels of economic growth—faced by workers and
communities all over the country that drives this work. That is, we are constantly hearing, from both the academic and popular press, that the economy is global and that capital is so mobile as to be able to go anywhere, at
any time, and at dizzying speeds. Mark Miller (the former editor of the
Berkshire Eagle) and I are therefore asking the relatively simple question:
What can people in localities *do* in the face of that mobile capital?

The second issue is embodied by Gramsci's typically incomprehensible
statement, which is about the inherent relationship between political theory
and political practice. You can't *do* political theory in the absence of practice

1

(Well, you can, but I would strongly argue that you can't do it well—that is, in a way that is useful to the political project you are supporting). This book is therefore a deliberate attempt to bridge academic theory and the often much messier contexts, conflicts, and situations encountered by those working to change the world that the theory is attempting to explain.

But Gramsci's argument goes beyond this to say that we need an agenda to realize political victory, and, at the same time, that agenda can only become apparent to us if we are part of the process of creating the institutions and structures that constitute it. Put more simply, "we can predict the future to the extent that we are involved in making it happen" (Katz, 1995, p. 167). To state the objectives of this book in the clearest possible language, they are to support and promote the construction of a more equitable and just world than the one we currently live in, and to allow people, living and working at the local level, to have greater control over the economic processes, structures, and institutions that shape and govern their lives. This is *the future* I would like to see. And this book, which emerged out of a period of prolonged engagement with, and participation in, different struggles to make that future happen, is a deliberate attempt to help in the formulation of that program.

These two quotes are, therefore, mutually informing. This is because creating conditions of local control is not an end in-and-of-itself but is instead a desirable outcome only if the conditions created are part of the process of constructing more equitable cities and spaces in which people live and work. Local autonomy (local control) is only a means to an end, the end being to transform the power relations that currently structure our political economy. Inherent in that goal is creating economic institutions that are participatory and democratic, and having that democratic control be exerted at the local level. This is not a hypothetical proposition. Nor is it based on a vision of some utopia completely divorced from reality and the world we live in. There are forms of localized ownership that have been created in the United States. And these forms of localized ownership have often been created with these goals in mind. The empirical and political questions remain, however, of how much they engender local control and how equitable the relations are within them.

Therefore these are the two primary themes of this book. First, it is an examination of the potential and possibility of local autonomy in the current political economic context of capital mobility, neoliberalism,[1] and economic globalization. Second, it is an exploration of whether the structures of local autonomy can equitably improve the lives of people in those localities. These themes come together with the explicit recognition and normative understanding that people should not be powerless in their interactions with the institutions that structure daily life. There should be, in short, a local and community basis to economic structures and relations.

Why Construct a Local Basis for Economic Relations?

There are several reasons why questions of local autonomy and capital mobility need to be addressed in a work concerned principally with issues of equity and justice. These range from the economic and political, to the moral and ethical. Regarding economics, the argument presented here goes very much against the grain of mainstream economic thinking. Mainstream economics, with its goals of efficiency and the promotion of profits and shareholder interests, has no place for notions of *place or community*. If capital mobility is the greatest way to realize profits and to operate efficiently in the market, then capital mobility should not be impeded by governments or other extra-economic actors. For while economics acknowledges that capital mobility might be a bit disconcerting for some localities at particular times (if that is acknowledged at all), the general assumption is that economic efficiency is the goal that trumps all others in a society's pursuit of wealth and prosperity. This view was probably made most explicit by Milton Friedman in his extremely influential article in the *New York Times Magazine*, where he bluntly stated that, "There is one and only one social responsibility of business—to use its resources and engage in activities designed to increase its profits" (Friedman, 1970, p. 125).

But what the mainstream economic perspective fails to understand is that the processes of capital mobility and economic globalization are not free of economic costs. Capital mobility is, in many ways, economically inefficient. This is because it destroys the worth of investments fixed in places, by making those investments no longer able to reproduce capital, and thus, ultimately, no longer forms of capital at all. Some of these dead capital investments are private, intrafirm costs—and therefore factored into businesses decisions to move—but a substantial amount of the capital destroyed has been invested by the public sector. These public investments come in a host of forms, including the basic infrastructure for the production process (such as roads, utilities, etc.), and the costs of socially producing and reproducing the labor of the workers (through public expenditures in education, housing, health care, etc.). When a company chooses to relocate, or bank or real-estate firm decides to invest elsewhere, these public investments are made redundant. This is why some local governments in the 1980s began using their powers of eminent domain to prevent plant closures (Weinberg, 1984), and why certain industrial communities have come to look at industrial property as if it is the community's, and not the capitalist's (Lynd, 1997, ch. 10). Recently, there has been a growing interest in the possibility of quantifying the exact costs borne by the public sector in dealing with capital mobility (Williamson, Imbroscio, and Alperovitz, 2002).

But perhaps the most significant economic argument against the current regime of neoliberal globalization and capital mobility is that it is simply not working for large numbers of people in the United States. Despite a period of protracted aggregate economic growth, by the turn of the century, most low-income, and many middle-income, people were still struggling to meet the basic needs of human beings. This can be seen in terms of workers' wages, housing costs, and access to basic human services like health care. I don't want to dwell too much on this here, because, despite the mainstream media's blackout of the problems facing low-income people and communities (Goozner, 2000), this reality is still fairly well known. A few key statistics should demonstrate my point. When it comes to income and wealth, American society is increasingly defined by growing inequalities—and not just because the rich are getting richer faster than everyone else, but because the middle class and low-income people have stagnated or declined. According to a study by the Congressional Budget Office, mean after-tax income for the bottom fifth of wage earners *fell* $100 a year (in inflation-adjusted dollars) from 1979 to 1997. Over that same period, mean after-tax income for the highest one percent grew by an astonishing $414,000 a year (Shapiro, Greenstein, and Primus, 2001). That study went on to find that:

> The top 20 percent of the population received half of the nation's after-tax income in 1997, the remaining 80 percent of the population shared the other half. The share of after-tax income received by each of the bottom four-fifths of the population fell from 1979 to 1997 (p. 6).

Similarly, mean family wealth holdings (which includes property, savings, stocks, bonds, etc.) for the bottom fifth of the population registered a 76.3-percent *loss* from 1983 to 1998, while for the top 20 percent, it climbed 30.3 percent over that same period (Wolff, 2000). Regarding housing, the data are not any better, and a study from the U.S. Department of Housing and Urban Development (HUD) found that from 1991 to 1997 the number of households facing a "Worst Case Housing" situation[2] grew by 12 percent (U.S. Department of Housing and Urban Development, 2000). Similarly, in 1998 over *one-third* of all renters paid more than 30 percent of their income in rent (National Low Income Housing Coalition, 1998). Finally, every year approximately 2 million men, women, and children in the United States experience some form of homelessness. Of these, 25 percent are children, meaning there are about *half a million* homeless children in this country every year (National Law Center on Homelessness and Poverty, 1999). And these numbers grew in the 1990s, despite, or perhaps because of, the aggregate economic growth. I could continue and present a mountain of empirical evidence to continue making this point, but it is probably not necessary. In short, the American economic system of neoliberalism, capital mobility, and globalization, isn't working for large numbers of American people.

I recognize, of course, that I'm conflating different kinds of processes in this discussion. Capital mobility is not the same thing as economic globalization, and neither of them is the same as the government cutbacks and privatization that are the hallmarks of neoliberalism. There are certainly places in the world where globalization, capital mobility, and state retrenchment are divorced from each other—and the examples of the strong welfare states in Scandinavia and "communist" local governments in Emilia-Romagna in Italy come to mind. But these three political-economic processes have proceeded together in the US to such an extent that disentangling them is theoretically, empirically, and politically exceedingly difficult to do. Thus the economic arguments here address them as the united front that they are in American public policy, discourse, and life.

Aside from all of the economic reasons why the current form of neoliberal capitalism, with its attendant processes of capital mobility and globalization, should be rejected, there are also several political and moral issues involved as well. First, the costs of capital mobility are paid for by the public sector, and the benefits, in terms of shareholder values and corporate profits, are realized by a few private individuals. The process of capital mobility, therefore, needs to be understood as a redistribution of wealth from society as a whole to the limited number of individuals who are able to realize wealth from that mobility. It may be that this political redistribution of capital is a conscious process, and the outcome of a nationwide political debate. But I certainly cannot recall there being one. Instead, this redistribution is a largely invisible process, which, in the context of the vitriolic political arguments of the last twenty years against the redistribution of wealth, and the creation of the infamously iconic status of "welfare queens" and other "sponges off of society," has gone remarkably unmentioned. This redistribution of wealth (of the public sector paying the costs for decisions that are made by, and benefit, a few private individuals), I should add, is on top of the various, and more direct, public subsidies businesses that are mobile, or threaten mobility, receive from local and state governments.

Second, there is a basic issue of democracy and democratic governance that needs to be addressed here. That is, as political philosophers have long argued, people learn and construct democracy by participating in democracy (see Pateman, 1970, for an excellent explanation of this). In American society, that process of participating in, and constructing, democracy has always been, first and foremost, experienced and realized at the community and local levels (see de Tocqueville, 1969 [1835], for the most famous analysis of this). Thus the inability of people acting at the local level to exert control over the basic structures that govern their lives raises vital questions for the future of even the notion of a democratic society in the United States. It is little wonder that voter participation rates have plummeted in the last thirty years—the global political economy has undercut the ability of people to act meaningfully (that is, with any potential influence) at precisely the geographic and social scales at which democracy is created.

Finally, this scale argument can be taken one step further. Despite the rhetoric of hypermobility and globalization, and despite the transformative role that this current period of immigration has had on American society, most people still live very localized existences. As Doreen Massey simply, and usefully, put it, "Much of life for people, even in the heart of the First World, still consists of waiting in a bus-shelter with your shopping for a bus that never comes" (Massey, 1994, p. 163). That is, people still live and work and interact with their families and friends in very localized settings. And while those experiences are necessarily enmeshed in much larger-scale relationships, it is still at the local level where they are felt. This is particularly true for poor and working class people. As British journalist Judith Williamson put it:

> Some people, in effect, are more "local" than others, and this is, fundamentally, a class issue. If you live in private housing, have a car, send your children to private schools (or have none) the council [local government] may seem to do little except empty your bins. If you are, say, a council tenant, elderly, with no car, your life is lived very locally indeed (Williamson, 2002).

Given this reality, it is the argument of this book that people should have some say and control over the experiences of their daily lives. Otherwise, we have taken the Marxian notion of alienation and extended it to virtually all realms of our social and cultural, as well as our workplace, lives. In short, it is the basic democratic goal of self-determination that is at stake here. That, ultimately, is why this book is joining the ranks of those calling for greater local control over economic structures and relationships.

Now all of this could be dismissed as some absurd Quixotic effort, struggling against the world and natural processes of capital mobility and neoliberal economic globalization. But capital mobility and the current form of economic globalization are not a natural, pregiven state of affairs. By this I mean three, interrelated things. First, the organization of economic activity is never natural. There is nothing more natural about neoliberal capitalism than there was about the Keynesian welfare state or the Soviet state-managed economy—or, for that matter, mercantilism, slavery, feudalism, etc. Instead, any form of economic organization is constructed through social relationships, and dialectically, acts to construct those social relationships in ways that both reproduce the economy, and, at times, potentially undermine it. The point is that the economy is inherently socially and politically created. Any understandings to the contrary are, at best misguided, or, at worst, politically oppressive.

Second, globalization and capital mobility are processes, they are not static end products. The economic realities that we are confronting right now are not, in any sense, a done deal. *The Economist*, the weekly bible of neoclassical economics, understands this point very well, and is thus terrified of the nascent social movement that has emerged since the late 1999 Seattle/WTO protests. On the eve of the Prague World Bank/International Monetary Fund (IMF) talks/protests, its lead commentary was called "The Case For Globalisation" and is worth quoting at length, as it stated:

> International economic integration is not an ineluctable process, as many of its most enthusiastic advocates appear to believe. It is only one, the best, of many possible futures for the world economy; others may be chosen, and are even coming to seem more likely. Governments, and through them their electorates, will have a far bigger say in deciding this future than most people appear to think. The protesters are right that governments and companies—if only they can be moved by force of argument, or just by force—have it within their power to slow and even reverse the economic trends of the past 20 years (*The Economist*, 2000).

But the best evidence of the tenuous hold that neoliberal globalization has on the world comes not from the protesters, or astute neoclassical economists, but from the economic history of the world. When one looks at the period in which trade played the largest role in the world's economy, it is actually in the period from the 1880s to 1914—not the period since the early 1970s (Dicken, 1998; Hirst and Thompson, 1996). We've been down this road before, and it only took the assassination of an archduke in the Balkans to start World War I and trigger a set of worldwide decisions to turn away from it. Surely the exploitation and oppression of the majority of the world's people that is inherently part of neoliberal globalization provides the potential for more substantial triggers than that.

Third, not only are capital mobility and globalization processes, but they are processes that are constructed through a very deliberate set of political actions that facilitate and promote them. *We* produce globalization. We produce it through our employment and our consumption, but, vitally, also through the actions of our states. The reason why the World Trade Organization was established is because the processes of globalization need governance by public sector apparatuses. We don't just politically produce globalization at the global scale, but also do so through political decisions made at the national, state, and local levels. The *global* does not exist prior to the local or national, but largely because of the national and local.

Thus, local autonomy is a theoretically realizable goal to which we should aspire. But if we accept this argument, then the questions become, what *is* local autonomy? And how might it be realized? In particular, how can local autonomy be realized in the face of capital mobility and the global economy?

Capital Mobility, Local Autonomy, and the NUP

A common academic and public policy understanding of capital mobility is that it has rendered localities virtually powerless in the face of that mobility. Since capital can go anywhere, the argument goes, all localities can do is try to attract that capital to come to them. This "New Urban Politics" (NUP) has seen city governments cut social services, invest public money directly in economic development projects, and promote downtown development as their principal objective. In this view, the flows of investment capital are seen as almost noncorporeal and placeless, while cities are trapped by their location. Perhaps the best-known articulation of this view came from Castells (1989), when he depressingly described the current global political economy as being characterized by a situation of "placeless power vs. powerless place."

Along a different line, there has been a lot of theoretical work done in both the UK and the U.S. on local autonomy, but most of this work is rather static in its interpretations of both locality and autonomy. Locality is usually assumed to correspond to the scale of the local state, and autonomy is understood as a set of delineated rights and responsibilities that local governments either do or do not possess. Local autonomy, therefore, is usually understood as the ability of local governments to act in isolation from outside constraints or influences in the realm of public policy.

I am arguing, conversely, for much more relational and process-oriented understandings of both locality and autonomy. A locality is not a thing, but is instead a set of relatively shared experiences and perspectives. It is a "common sense" produced through the internal and external relationships in which those within a place are embedded. Autonomy, similarly, is a form of power, and therefore not a discrete entity possessed by any person or institution. Instead autonomy is a set of relationships that the person or institution is able to control. So local autonomy is not about localities being able to act in isolation from outside forces. Instead, local autonomy is realized when actors within localities have recognized how they are connected to the extralocal world, and have transformed those connections so that they are better able to control them.

In terms of capital mobility and the NUP, what this means is that localities need to transform the relationships between capital and the other actors in places. In spite of claims to the contrary, capital is not placeless but—some forms of it appear to be so because they are able to operate at scales larger than any single locality, region, or nation. To realize autonomy, people acting locally need to transform the scale at which capital operates, and make that capital place-bound when it otherwise wouldn't be. The most obvious way to do this is to own the forms of capital accumulation directly within the locality. There are two ways to create ownership of capital that render capital immobile. One is by owning capital through an organization or institution, which is defined by place, and therefore place-bound (like a municipal government or community-based organization). The other is by creating a localized collective ownership structure. For while individual owners might relocate, die, or retire, a collective of owners is not particularly likely to do so.

There are certainly some people who, because of their class and race position, are already able to realize autonomy in many of their relations and interactions with the rest of the world—and the proliferation of "gated communities" in the U.S. is a striking expression of this (and also a striking example of why community control should not be the goal in and of itself, but only a goal insomuch as it is infused with a sense of social justice and equity; gated communities, defined as they are by exclusion, are clearly not the model for equitable urbanization). But for many people in the US, who lack these structurally created bases of collective and individual power, action is needed at the community or local level to realize some degree of control or autonomy in their lives.

Community Control and Collective Ownership

These are, of course, not particularly new solutions. There is a long history in the United States of people making this same argument and implementing forms of collective ownership in order to realize local control. The earliest forms of this emerged in the early nineteenth century when various communes were established throughout the country with a variety of political objectives. This tradition was "rediscovered" in the 1960s (although it had continued in various forms throughout the nineteenth and twentieth centuries). This rediscovery emerged from both the movement for black power and the desire for "counterinstitutions" in the "New Left." The reemergence of collective ownership in the 1960s, however, was rather short-lived and the organizations that created it, in a plethora of forms, largely disappeared or were transformed into more traditional institutions during the 1970s and 1980s.

Ironically, while the collectives of the 1960s were dying out, the processes of capital mobility were generating a new set of collectively owned entities (see Bruyn and Meehan, 1987; DeFilippis, 1999; Douthwaite, 1996; Gunn and Gunn, 1991; Shavelson, 1990; Shuman, 1998; Wilkenson and Quarter, 1996). Unlike many of the earlier groups, these organizations were largely formed in response to specific crises and struggles, and were therefore often not due to a larger vision for society. The crises ranged from plant closures by multinational corporations, to neighborhood disinvestment existing side-by-side with downtown renewal or neighborhood reinvestment in the form of gentrification and the war against the poor, to the continuing practice of redlining or the problem of neighborhood bank branch closures as part of larger-scale financial institution restructuring. The responses to these crises and conflicts were to create forms of collective ownership because, it was theorized, collective ownership would "root capital to place" in ways that individual ownership did not. These collectives have arrived at the very same conclusions that I just briefly spelled out here. That is, if low income and working people want more control over their lives, they need to create forms of ownership and governance that allow them to realize that control.

These localized responses, which some activists/authors have referred to as "the Lilliput Strategy" (Brecher and Costello, 1994; Brecher, Costello, and Smith, 2000; Shuman, 1998) are the object of study here. They vary considerably, but for the sake of simplification I have placed them into three different categories of ownership based on the social and economic spheres in which they operate. These are:

   I.   Collective Ownership of Work
  II.   Collective Ownership of Housing
 III.   Collective Ownership of Money

These three forms of ownership correspond to the three dominant realms of socio-economic relations in people's lives under capitalism. People need to work, sleep, eat and live, and consume in their daily lives. If localities emerge out of the common sense that comes from daily, experiential practices, then the potential for both local autonomy and social transformation hinge on the ability of those within localities to appropriate control over the structures and institutions that are the focal points of those experiences and practices. Collective ownership of work refers to workers owning their site of employment, and, of the three types discussed here, it is probably the best known. It generally takes one of two forms: Employee Stock Ownership Plans, or worker cooperatives. Collective ownership of housing can occur in several different ways, but the most common forms are limited-equity housing cooperatives, community land trusts, and mutual housing associations. Collective ownership of money refers to forms of financial institutions that are owned by the people whose capital constitutes those institutions. I recognize that these categories are crude and oversimplify a lot, but the need for organization and structure in political and scholarly work sometimes requires forms of strategic simplification.

Questions for This Book

Beyond the two core themes of this book, there are several other issues that run throughout it. First is the question of how feasible are forms of localized collective ownership in the contemporary global political economy. Collectives have been, and are being, created, but there remains the question of how easily replicable they are. I will argue that such collectives are replicable, but the political will to create, and fully understand them needs to be generated. The second theme addressed is whether or not these collectives demonstrably, and equitably, improve the lives of the people within them. For if they fail to do this, then there is little point in promoting them. I will present evidence that these forms of collectives certainly do improve the lives of people involved in them. To some extent this is because these collectives largely emerge as a result of localized expressions of the failure of the market to provide basic components of people's lives (such as housing, employment, credit). The collectives are largely born out of crisis, in which the people involved usually have no other choice (but to act collectively), and therefore the collectives, almost by virtue of their existence, represent an improvement in the lives of their members. But this improvement also results from the fact that the members are engaged in the collectives' decision-making processes, and are therefore able to look out for their own interests within the collectives.

The third theme is whether or not these forms of collective ownership allow for greater local control in localities' relations with the larger, supralocal world. That is, is collective ownership a vehicle for realizing local autonomy in the global economy? There are two parts to this theme. First, does collective ownership limit the mobility of capital? I argue that the collectives do indeed limit the mobility of capital, but they do not render the capital completely place-bound and immobile. Second, does that relative immobility engender local control? This issue is much messier and the results are mixed. The collectives do allow local actors to have much more control over the sector or commodity collectivized. But, generally speaking, the collectives are too small in size and the political and economic relationships that create localities are too diverse and disparate for local-scale actors to completely realize autonomy and control over their own localities. There is an ambivalence about the potential of these forms of collectives that runs through the book. This is not a celebration of these efforts (like, for instance, Shuman's [1998] book is). These are not wonder institutions, and the expectations for them must be realistic. Their potential lies in what they represent, and the potential for greater local autonomy that is possible, rather than in what they are actually able to achieve given their limited size and capacity at this time.

The fourth theme of the book is a critique of community development practices as they have evolved over the last thirty-five years. This project is not simply a product of capital mobility and neoliberal globalization. It is also a result of a growing sense of frustration I have with the trajectory of community development theory and practice. Increasingly, the community development world has accepted the individualist/free market/small government perspectives of the dominant, neoliberal political economy. This book, conversely, argues that *community* development requires a collective, rather than individual, emphasis in low-income neighborhoods and localities. It also argues that embracing the market by those practicing community development ignores the historic role of the market in producing the underdevelopment of their communities. It maintains that such a promarket turn also leaves the power relations that produce communities and localities, and in which the market controls the patterns of investment and disinvestment, unaltered.

The final theme of this work is the issue of transformative practices. That is, does collective ownership have the potential to transform the structures and institutions of the American political economy? To some extent, this is an unrealizable goal to set for these scattered and localized forms of ownership. However, this is a vital question, and it rests on the distinction between a practice that simply happens to be alternative and one that is consciously and reflexively oppositional. Oppositional efforts may not have the capacity to be socially transformative, but alternatives that remain as such are exceedingly unlikely to be—simply because that is not their goal. Alternatives can become transformative if they self-reflectively operate with a different set of goals and logics than those that dominate. But once that reflection occurs, and is acted upon, then what was once simply alternative becomes oppositional.

As suggested earlier, the collective forms of ownership here emerged within the margins of capitalism, spaces where capital had chosen not to invest. This can limit the political and economic impact of such collectives, and thus their transformative potential. But spaces which are marginal to capital inherently exist in the flows of investment within the capitalist economy, and it is in precisely such margins, or, what Michael Mann (1986) calls, "interstitial locations" where alternative forms of ownership, control, and capital accumulation can most easily be created. Uneven development and "cores" and "peripheries" are inherently part of how capitalism operates in and through geographic space. Why not use that reality of capitalism to construct oppositional alternatives to it?

Outline of the Book

Beyond this introduction, this book is divided into six chapters and an epilogue. Chapter 1 gets to the heart of the questions of this project by dealing with recent transformations in the global political economy, and the emergence of a "New Urban Politics" (NUP) that is both a product, and producer, of that global economy. It briefly discusses the impacts of these changes on poor and working communities in the United States. It then discusses how local governments have been acting in the current regime of accumulation, and explores the transformation of local politics from issues of local govern*ments* to those of local gover*nance*. This chapter also presents a theoretical argument as to why local autonomy needs to be reconceptualized, particularly in the context of economic globalization and capital mobility. Accordingly, it presents a framework for how we can understand local autonomy in the global political economy. It concludes by presenting a general discussion of the groups and organizations that are working to operationalize this understanding of local autonomy.

Chapter 2 presents the historical roots of efforts at collective ownership and community control in the United States. It begins with the various communes in the early nineteenth century, and their diverse foundations (in race, religion, rural populism, etc.). From there, the chapter describes the experience of the collectives and communes created during the 1960s. The chapter then shifts gears a bit and presents the political and ideological transformations of community organizing and community development from the 1960s to the present. Over this period, notions of "community control," a mantra of black power and radicalism in the 1960s, have been supplanted by the increasingly less explicitly political, and more market-based, goals of "capacity-building," "asset-based development," and "social capital construction." In short, this historical process is dominated by the loss of both the radical political component of the work of people involved in community development, and community development's social movement roots. This has left the community development "movement," or, much more accurately, "industry," and its infrastructure, unable to either organize politically, or to use the alternative, and collective, models of ownership formed by some within it, to generate a systemic political critique.

In chapters 3, 4, and 5, the book moves from the theoretical and historical to the applied and contemporary. They discuss attempts to use collective ownership to create local control over the means of production, reproduction, and exchange, respectively. Each chapter contains a general discussion of the problems facing low-income and working-class communities in each realm of activity under the current regime of capital accumulation. They then move on to discuss organizations and movements created to establish collective forms of ownership, as ways of dealing with the inequities and failures of this regime. Data are therefore provided to demonstrate the growth and vitality of such collective forms of ownership. In order to illuminate the issues, tensions, problems, and conflicts evident in these collectives, each chapter also includes short case studies. These cases are very Northeast U.S.–centric. That is perhaps justifiable given that I am a New Yorker who has lived and worked most of my life here—and this book is largely about the importance of "the local" in social and political life. But this is a bias that must be recognized, given that the Northeast is politically very different from most of the rest of the United States. These cases were also chosen because they are recognized as successful by those within their respective sectors. While this is an inherent bias—and it could be claimed that they are "anomalous"—the point of this book is to demonstrate the potential of these forms of ownership, and therefore I needed to select groups that exhibit that potential. The chapters end with discussions that evaluate the potential and limits of the particular form of collective ownership examined.

Chapter 3 begins with a discussion of the issues of industrial transformation and the ability of industrial capital to use its mobility to wreak havoc on the lives of the relatively place-bound working-class people in industrial employment. It then discusses the history, politics, and economic viability of worker-ownership, and focuses on the transformation of worker-ownership from an issue of workplace relations and the market for equity shares, to an issue of capital mobility, geographic scale, and local control. It documents the growth of worker-ownership, and the uses of worker buyouts of worksites threatened with disinvestment or closure. The chapter then briefly presents the case of Cooperative Health Care Associates (CHCA). CHCA is a worker-cooperative of home health-care workers in the Bronx, New York. This is followed by the much larger case study of Marland Mold, Inc. Marland Mold is a factory in Pittsfield, Massachusetts, that was threatened with plant closure as part of the industrial corporate restructuring of the early 1990s. Instead of falling victim to that restructuring, the workers bought their company, and have thrived ever since. The chapter concludes by addressing the economic and political potential of worker ownership in the United States.

Chapter 4 commences with a discussion of the processes of disinvestment and reinvestment in inner-city housing in the United States. It focuses on gentrification as a process which demonstrates that the problems in disinvested areas are not simply a lack of capital, but a lack of control over capital investment (since the residents of gentrified areas are usually displaced by the reinvestment process). It then discusses the history and politics of low-income cooperatives, and describes the emergence and proliferation of Limited-Equity Housing Co-operatives, Mutual Housing Associations, and Community Land Trusts. These are forms of not-for-profit housing in which the housing units (or the property they are on) have been removed from the marketplace and are owned collectively. Because the housing is no longer a commodity, it is therefore protected from the market processes of either disinvestment and housing stock decay or reinvestment in the form of gentrification and displacement. It then briefly describes the experiences of the limited-equity co-ops in the Lower East Side of New York, and the Burlington Community Land Trust in Burlington, Vermont. This is followed by a more in-depth case study of the Mutual Housing Association of Southwestern Connecticut. The Mutual Housing Association of Southwestern Connecticut was created in the late 1980s in a low-income neighborhood in Stamford that had suffered from long-term disinvestment, but was also facing substantial gentrification pressures. The chapter concludes by focusing on the barriers and opportunities inherent in cooperative housing efforts.

Chapter 5 starts by describing the growth of financial institutions as one of the primary mechanisms in the creation and reproduction of the contemporary political economy. It documents how, as financial capital has grown, it has become increasingly disassociated from the communities and localities in which people, particularly low-income and nonwhite people, live. It then describes the history, and growth, of Local Exchange Trading Systems (LETS) and presents the brief case of Ithaca Hours, a form of LETS in Ithaca, New York. The chapter then discusses community development financial institutions (CDFIs), which are financial institutions that work to redirect capital back into underserved areas. It then focuses on community development credit unions (CDCUs), which, of all the CDFIs are the only ones that are collectively owned. It then discusses the experiences of Bethex Federal Credit Union in the South Bronx. The chapter ends with a discussion of the political and economic potential of LETS, credit unions, and the efforts to locally control the processes and structures of exchange.

Chapter 6 will bring together the experiences of the different forms of collectives discussed in the preceding chapters and will return to the themes of local politics, local autonomy, and social transformation evident throughout the work. It will highlight the potential and limitations of collective ownership, and, in so doing, illuminate new directions for the theory and practice of local and community-based economic development in an era of capital mobility and economic globalization.

As this research was being completed, and while it was being written, a set of protests, beginning in Seattle at the meetings of the World Trade Organization and moving on from there, have transformed the public conversation about globalization in the United States. Unfortunately, the activists and protestors have too often failed to connect with community-based organizations in the United States. This failure has been a two-way process. The anti–neoliberal globalization protestors have prioritized direct actions at international events at the expense of other, more localized, forms of organizing. Community-based organizations, as I have indicated above, have turned away from explicitly critical or radical politics, and have therefore largely passed on participating in the demonstrations. This short epilogue will discuss this disjuncture in the context of the proceeding analysis, and point toward ways in which local and community organizations working for social change can connect with their newly globalized counterparts.

CHAPTER 1

Understanding Capital Mobility, the "New Urban Politics," and Local Autonomy[1]

The key fact of our historical moment is said to be the globalization of national economies . . . I don't think this explanation is entirely wrong but it is deployed so sweepingly as to be misleading. And right or wrong, the explanation itself has become a political force, helping to create the institutional realities it purportedly merely describes.
—Frances Fox Piven, 1995

The last twenty-five years have seen a radical transformation in the structures and relationships that govern the capitalist political economy. [1] Economic relations have become increasingly globalized, and investment capital has become increasingly footloose and mobile. While there is nothing new about making these statements, it is this political and economic restructuring that has given rise to this book, and consequently it needs to be addressed. This chapter will begin by briefly discussing the economic debates that have surrounded the issues of capital mobility and globalization, and draw out the commonalities in the assumptions of researchers and policy makers within these debates. From there, the chapter deals with the political implications of these economic changes, and specifically how the global economy has transformed, and, in turn, been transformed by, changes in local politics and urban governance. These changes in local politics are analyzed through the lens of questions of local autonomy. Accordingly, the chapter critiques the theoretical understandings most common in works on local autonomy, and presents a reconstruction of this theory. It concludes by briefly introducing organizations and people working in their localities to realize local autonomy in the face of the global political economy.

Economic Restructuring and Capital Mobility

The American, and global, political economy of the last quarter of the twentieth century was dominated by the transformation of relations between capital and workers and communities. This process of restructuring has been constituted by a set of new relationships and institutional forms, and it has been accompanied by a mini-industry of research by social scientists and policy makers who have struggled to decipher its causes, forms, and implications. It is not the goal of this book to thoroughly summarize or examine these literatures, since that has been done elsewhere (see, for instance, Brecher and Costello, 1994; Dicken, 1998; Lee and Wills, 1999; Moody, 1997; Reich, 1991; Storper, 1997). Instead, I will only briefly discuss the points of common agreement before introducing some of the most important ways in which this restructuring is important for this work.

Despite the diversity of perspectives and theories that have been put forward to understand and explain this period of economic restructuring, several shared theses are important for us here. First, there is general agreement that, beginning in the early 1970s and precipitated by the economic crises of the time, there has been a process of substantial economic restructuring that has transformed some of the basic relationships of the capitalist political economy. Second, there has been a radical break in the capitalist patterns of embeddedness and disembeddedness of investment, as certain forms of capital have become much more geographically mobile than they had ever been before. In short, the relationships between capital and the other actors that create places have been radically restructured. And capital is using its increased mobility to strengthen its position vis-à-vis those other actors (like the state, trade unions, community organizations, etc.).

Third, and greatly facilitating that capital mobility, the roles of producer services, and the producer services sectors, have grown dramatically relative to industrial capital and the industrial production sectors. This is an era dominated by the growth of the "FIRE" sectors—that is, Finance, Insurance, and Real Estate. Fourth, and similarly facilitating the mobility of capital, has been a growth of technological capabilities that have reduced the barriers of distance. This has principally been in the form of communication and information technologies, but is also true regarding the movement of tangible objects (and widespread containerization in shipping is the archetypal example of this).

Fifth, the scale of operations for larger firms has become supranational, and often global. This is the era of the transnational, and often multinational, corporation (MNC). And while MNCs have long existed in the world economy, it is through them, their incredible growth, and primarily their patterns of investment rather than trade, that the world economy is *globalizing*. Sixth, there is a new geography of regional growth, as older industrial regions (such as the Great Lakes region), and localities (such as Buffalo) have declined while new industrial regions emerged and developed (Silicon Valley and Route 128 outside of Boston being the archetypes of the new industrial regions), and new cities (such as Charlotte, North Carolina) grew and prospered.

Finally, the roles of the state in capitalism have been transformed as the Keynesian[2] model of state-capital-worker relations, which dominated from the 1930s to the 1970s, has receded and been replaced by a set of relations that are less likely to intervene on behalf of labor vis-à-vis capital. The state has, in short, gone from a Keynesian state, concerned with regulating and maintaining aggregate national demand via the distribution of wealth and a social welfare system, to a state focused on the supply of money in the economy and creating conditions that are favorable for capital investment (like low taxes, a docile labor force, etc.). This state restructuring is true for both the regulatory and distributive roles of the state in economics. While other countries, like the United Kingdom, have experienced a similar process of state restructuring, it has been particularly pronounced in the United States. All of these changes have left a very different political and economic landscape for the new century, and have raised real questions about the role of localities and local politics.

Entrepreneur Politics and Urban Economic Development Policies

In the context of these changes over the last twenty-five years, local politics and governments have become very different from what they had been. The process of state restructuring has therefore been experienced and felt at the local level as much as it has at the national or state levels. Rather than describe all of the particular changes, which has capably been done elsewhere (see, for instance, Clarke and Gaile, 1998; and Hall and Hubbard, 1998), this chapter will instead pull out the four key themes and trends that characterize the transformation of local politics and government in the era of globalization and capital mobility.

First, this is an era of intensified economic competition between cities. Economic competition between cities has long existed in the U.S., but this competition has increased in the last twenty-five years, and has involved new roles and initiatives on the part of local governments. While there are numerous causes of this increased competition, there is little doubt that because of the increased mobility of capital, cities are increasingly competing against each other to be the destinations for mobile capital—and, it should be added, to maintain the capital already located in places, and which might get lured away. As Kantor and David (1988, p. 229) put it:

> The tremendous mobility of capital forms the major barrier to local economic development. So long as localities cannot firmly tie many business enterprises to the community's infrastructure and labor force, intergovernmental competition pressures city governments to provide business incentives.[3]

This increased competition between localities has been heightened by the decline in transfers of money from the federal to municipal governments, which has made localities increasingly dependent upon self-generated revenue—and hence more economically competitive with each other. And while this competition is often more regional than global (see Kincaid, 1997), it is nonetheless capital mobility and the restructuring of the state that are the driving forces behind this process.

Second, there has accordingly been a shift in local government from being primarily concerned with issues of the local management of social services to being more explicitly and actively entrepreneurial in its goals and actions. Municipal governments have traditionally been concerned with the provision of the goods needed for social reproduction (or "collective consumption" as Castells [1977] put it) at the local level. This included schools, health care, housing, public safety, infrastructure, etc. Local governments continue to be involved in the provision of such goods, but they have significantly supplemented this work by becoming more directly involved in the processes of economic development within their localities. This shift, which Harvey (1989) referred to as, "From Managerialism to Entrepreneurialism" is perhaps the defining characteristic of contemporary urban politics and government. Many researchers have therefore talked about this period as one of a "New Urban Politics" (NUP). Significantly, this entrepreneurial turn has been embraced by both dominant parties. It was probably Arkansas governor and presidential candidate Bill Clinton who most forcefully brought the issue of the entrepreneurial state into the national discussion by openly embracing the work of David Osborne, who in his two books, *Laboratories of Democracy* (1990) and *Reinventing Government* (1992), championed the ideas of entrepreneurial government.

It is a bit of an oversimplification to argue that it is completely new for city governments to be involved in economic development issues, and municipal governments have long used tax credits or abatements and industrial revenue bonds (among other tools) to attract investment capital. But in the current entrepreneurial framework, city governments have become much more proactive in their efforts to generate local economic growth and development. Such entrepreneurial efforts have included business incubators, venture capital financing, revolving loan pools, joint (public and private) ventures in commercial real-estate development, etc. In short, rather than simply lowering the costs of doing business in the locality, local governments have increasingly become investors and risk takers—i.e., entrepreneurs—in the economic development within their localities.

Importantly, the data for the effectiveness of such entrepreneurial strategies has been mixed at best. Efforts at evaluation have been plagued by basic problems in defining the proper outcomes and assessing the goals of economic development. Such confusion over evaluation, mixed with a significant number of disaster stories of rather egregious forms of "corporate welfare" (see Queer Economic Justice Network, 2002, for an excellent discussion of the issues, and many cases, of corporate welfare) have cast a large pale over the success (by whatever measure) of entrepreneurial local governance. In their comprehensive review of the local economic development literature, Wolman with Spitzley (1999) even felt compelled to include an entire section devoted to, "Why Do They Do It, Even Though We Tell Them It Does Not Work?" (p. 242).

Third, local politics has become increasingly characterized by a shift away from local govern*ment* and toward local govern*ance*, as more and more activities and functions are performed outside of the specific structures of local governments. This shift, from the public sector to the quasi-public, private, or not-for-profit sectors has occurred in both the more traditional provision of social services, and the newer, more privatized and entrepreneurial activities of local governance. Social services are increasingly provided by not-for-profit (and, in some cases, for-profit) corporations, and affordable housing is overwhelmingly built by the nongovernment—rather than the public—sector. Similarly, business improvement districts (BIDs), have sprung up in seemingly every urban commercial center, and there are at least 400 operating in 42 states (Mitchell, 1999). BIDs are areas where the property owners have agreed to pay a fee, collected by city governments, but then returned directly to the BID boards—the local property owners—to be spent in the BID area, and to provide many of the functions, such as policing and sanitation, that had been the responsibility of local governments. As a result of all these changes, the provision of social services and housing have suffered as small, often community-based nongovernment organizations (NGOs) and not-for-profits struggle to fulfill the roles of local governments despite their usual lack of resources and capacity.

Finally, as a result of the above transformations, there are growing gaps between the different classes and races in American cities. When the shift of local politics away from social-service provision is combined with the decline in industrial employment and the growth in high-paying producer services and low-paying consumer-services jobs, we are left with a situation in which American cities are more unequal than they have been since the

1920s. This has led many observers to talk about the emergence of "Dual Cities" in the U.S. While this characterization might be bit too simplistic, there is a significant amount of truth in it. Perhaps more important than this outcome is the fact that poverty alleviation, and social justice more broadly, seem to have fallen off the urban political map. In a survey of local government officials, Furdell (1994) found that 48.2 percent stated that economic development was politically more important than poverty allevi-ation. Only 2.9 percent said the inverse. And Neil Smith has gone so far as to argue that contemporary urban politics are one of a "Revanchist City" (Smith, 1996) in which affluent and middle-class people are taking revenge upon the poor people and people of color that "took" the city from them in the post-war era. He might be overstating the case, but not by much.

Locality and Autonomy in the "New Urban Politics"

These then are the politics and policies that have dominated American urban life in the era of globalization. This is neither an unfamiliar story, nor a particularly optimistic one. I've already argued that these policies have demonstrated little aggregate economic benefits for the cities that employ them, and have had significantly negative impacts on poor people and people of color in American cities. But the question most important for this work—whether or not these new urban policies have enabled the possibility of meaningful local autonomy—remains unanswered. In order to address this, we need to take a step back and ask the prior questions of: What does local autonomy mean, and how might it be realized? Only then can we address the issues of local control and autonomy, and ultimately lo-cally based power in the global economy.

The arguments presented by planners, policy makers, and social scien-tists trying to understand the NUP are based on the assumption that since capital is increasingly global and mobile, localities are competing against each other more than ever before to attract this mobile capital. The conclu-sions drawn from this single, shared premise have varied greatly, however, and have ranged from arguments that cities have completely lost their au-tonomy relative to this newly mobile capital (Peterson, 1981; Gottdeiner, 1987; Kantor, 1995; Kantor with David, 1988; Logan and Molotch, 1987) to those that see a period of "new localism" as a result of this new mobility (Goetz and Clarke, 1993; Clarke and Gaile, 1998; Kanter, 1995).

Peterson (1981) was probably the first social scientist to explicitly ad-dress the implications of capital mobility on local politics, and his views have largely framed the debates since. He argued that capital and labor "vote with their feet" and use the economically rational priorities of taxes paid relative to benefits received to determine their location and residence.

Also, because capital and labor were mobile, and the United States has a federal state structure, which forces cities to rely on locally generated revenue, cities had *no choice* but to prioritize the "developmental" policies of economic growth. Comparable arguments would later be made, although from different normative and political positions, in two influential texts by both Gottdiener (1987) and Logan and Molotch (1987).

In reaction to, and against, the above "city limits" literature, another school of thought has emerged celebrating the importance of local politics in this global era. This "new localists" literature has essentially made two arguments. First, it has asserted, and demonstrated, that local variations in politics and policies are still possible, and in fact exist, in the era of capital mobility and neoliberal globalization. Local politics cannot simply be read off of larger-scale socio-economic processes and developments. Second, it has argued that the globalization of economic relations and the increased mobility of capital, rather than rendering place meaningless, has actually reasserted the importance of place-based characteristics—and therefore empowered local politics.

The first argument of the new localists is a compelling one, and local actors and institutions do continue to construct a variety of ways in which to promote economic development. They do so because different localities contain different mixes of people, institutions, traditions, and cultures. Places do choose different paths to realizing economic growth, and certainly Portland, Oregon, with its strict antisprawl zoning laws, could not be confused with Houston, Texas, with its almost complete lack of planning and zoning regulations of any kind.

The second argument made by the new localists is that the mobility of capital has diminished spatial barriers to investment, thereby reasserting the importance of place-based characteristics in investment decisions. Clarke (1993, page 4) makes this argument explicit when she states, "To the extent that new production processes are, in fact, characterized by organizations seeking specific industrial atmospheres and attempting to reduce external transaction costs, localities—not regions or nations—are in a position to facilitate the minimization of these costs."

There is certainly more truth in the "new localism" arguments than in the arguments proclaiming a "death of urban politics." Localities have been, *and continue to be*, vital arenas in which different paths toward economic development are chosen. But there is also a vital core truth in the city limits perspective that should not be dismissed. That is, local decisions are still based on the underlying, and overlying, assumptions of neoliberal economic policies and the processes of globalization. Decisions about how best to develop in the global economy might increasingly be taking place at local levels—although this is probably as much a function of government devolution, and limited federal government resources for cities in the last twenty years, as it is of capital mobility—but such decisions leave unchanged the larger terrain of that global economy. In fact, such local decisions do more than just leave that larger terrain unchanged—they actively produce it! We therefore need a less narrow and truncated view of "decisions" and realize that local autonomy is not simply a matter of productively fitting into the global economy, but instead is about controlling how the very interactions between the local and larger scales take place, on what kind of playing field, and with what rules and values. In short, the entire understanding of local autonomy in the global economy needs to be re-examined and retheorized.

Reconceptualizing Locality and Autonomy

Both of the NUP's conflicting conclusions—either the complete loss of local autonomy or the emergence of a period of "hyper" local autonomy—are inadequate because they fail to understand the nuances involved in realizing local autonomy. This failure, as I suggested above, leads to flawed political understandings that unnecessarily limit the scope of local politics and the potential to realize local autonomy. These debates, in short, are not merely academic, but have occurred in and through public policy. That is why they need to be recast and reconceptualized.

First, a locality is not a thing that exists a priori—that is, prior to, and independent of, human experience—as the NUP seems to assume. Localities are, conversely, continuously being constructed and reconstructed, both by their relationships with the rest of the world, and by the struggles that take place within them. Also, the NUP seems to accept "the local" as the scale of the local state. Accordingly, its theorists have assumed away questions of what constitutes and produces the local. But while government institutions play a very large role in producing localities, "the local" is not necessarily determined by any scale within the geographic division of labor of the state.

Similarly, autonomy is not a discrete commodity that is possessed, or not possessed, by individuals or localities. Instead autonomy is a set of power relations. A locality therefore cannot *have* autonomy, since autonomy can only be realized through the social, political, and economic relationships that those within the locality are engaged in with the extralocal world. These flawed understandings of locality and autonomy are at the heart of the failure of the NUP, and it is toward more coherent conceptions of these that this chapter now turns.

Locality

The scale of the locality has been theorized in many different, often conflicting, ways in the social sciences and urban planning in the last twenty years. Instead of summarizing this vast literature, I will simply pull out the parts that are most useful to my understanding of locality before I synthesize them into a working definition.

Taylor (1982) defines locality as the "scale of experience," and Agnew (1987) would later expand this notion into "locale," as a way of trying to understand local political behavior. The idea of locale is that individuals live their lives in a place or setting, and that setting, as the site for many of their daily experiences, constrains and influences their behavior. The experiential component of this understanding of locality was made most explicit by Clarke and Kirby (1990), who describe locality as the scale where, a "common sense" is formed by those within it. It should be stressed, however, that this formation of a "common sense" within a place doesn't just happen, but is actively constructed and usually the result of unequal power relations within that place. Clarke and Kirby further argue for an understanding of locality as "a nexus of community, household, and workplace, which are essential components of everyday life and crucial organizations that shape political values and ideology" (Clarke and Kirby, 1990, p 394). The local, therefore, is the scale of lived experiences. As such, it is not fixed at any dimension (be it the scale of city government or the neighborhood or the metropolitan area) but varies in size and location for different people. A suburbanite, for instance, who lives and works in the same, or adjacent, suburbs, but never goes into the central city, does not have the central city in their locality. Though a neighbor who commutes to work in the city every day certainly does.

But locality is not completely amorphous, and even though state structures do not define localities, political boundaries are central to their constitution. This is so for two interrelated reasons. On one level, the state is an important part of the set of our daily experiences, and most people's interactions with the state occur at the local scale (whether it is with the police, schools, social service providers, etc.). Additionally, the state is not fixed itself, but is the codification of power relations. Thus the local state is one of the central structures in people's daily lives and experiences, and, as such, it becomes one of the primary arenas in which contests over people's "common sense" get played out.

There is something intuitively powerful about this conception of locality, but it fails to adequately explain the connections between lived experiences and the production of the locality. It doesn't, in short, tell us *how* a common sense in a place is formed.

In his seminal work on *The Production of Space*, Henri Lefebvre (1991) argued that places are constructed through social and political relations that occur along three interconnected axes. The first, *spatial practice*, refers to how people live their daily lives—that is, how people go to work, what kind of house they live in, where they shop for food, etc. The second, *representations of space*, is how space and places are conceived and conceptualized by those able to design, invest in, and construct the places and spaces in which we live our daily lives. This is space as it is seen by a city planner, a real-estate developer, an architect, etc. As Lefebvre bluntly states, "This is the dominant space in any society (or mode of production)" (Lefebvre, 1991, pp. 38–39, parentheses in original). Finally, there is *representational spaces*, which is how spaces and places are perceived, experienced, and truly *lived* (rather than just the actual physical activities that people engage in). Together these three axes combine, conflict, and intersect to produce the places in which we live and work. The importance of the last axis is to make explicit that places are not prefigured in their meanings to the people that use them. People, therefore, can transform places not simply by physically reorganizing them, but also by ascribing new meanings to them. To make this less theoretical, an example that demonstrates this point would be that of a worker buyout of a factory. The physical structure of the plant might not change at all, and workers might even go through many of the same daily practices (commuting on the same roads, eating the same food in the same cafeteria, etc.) as before the buyout, but the meanings and implications of the workplace have been significantly restructured. However, Lefebvre's explanation is incredibly abstract, and is more useful as a broad framework for understanding that places are socially produced than for more immediate political or empirical projects.

Along a different, and slightly less abstract line, Massey has argued that localities are moments in the "stretching out of social relations." In this framework, places emerge out of a geographically larger, or supralocal, set of relationships. Localities are therefore partially defined by their location in their relationships with the outside world, as well as the relationships that exist within them. In Massey's early work (1984), these relationships were primarily economic, and places were a product of their location within the spatial division of labor. This was, and is, an extremely important argument against the mainstream liberal and conservative understandings of poverty in cities or regions as a function of the qualities of the people within them (e.g., the lack of education to liberals, or "the culture of poverty" to conservatives). Despite this utility, it was also a very limiting framework and it reduced places to simply products of their historical economic geography. More recently, Massey (1994) has broadened her understanding of the production of places to include gender and race relations as well. Further sets of relations in the production of places can certainly be identified, but the point should already be clear: Localities are not simply products of the actions and characteristics of people and institutions within them. Instead, localities are produced through a complex set of actions and relationships—both by people that live in them and by those that do not. To paraphrase Massey, this begs the question of, "In what sense are local problems, really *local*?" Still, it remains unclear as to how all these relationships translate into the daily practices and experiences that constitute a locality.

Kevin Cox has worked through a helpful framework here (Cox and Mair, 1988, 1989; Cox, 1993, 1995) and has suggested the idea of locality as a function of the "locally dependent" structures, agents, and institutions that exist within it. In short, there are certain social relations and certain actors that simply *need* to be in a place, and for whom mobility, while often technically possible in this age of hypermobility, is de facto not an option. Therefore these actors are reliant, or "dependent" on the conditions of that place for the realization of their self-interests—whatever those interests might be. So while everything is relationally produced, it's not the same as saying that everything is mobile. The primary example is of capitals invested in a place, that, in order to recoup their initial investment, need to continue to have value flow through them—property owners being the archetypal examples of this, since real-estate property is fixed in place and cannot move. Small retail businesses are also both a substantial part of people's daily lives and relatively place-bound. They are also extremely important in urban economics. A recent study by Power found that the majority of U.S. economic activity "is local and provides residents with the goods and services that make their lives comfortable . . . local economies are dominated by residents taking in each other's wash" (quoted in Williamson, Imbroscio, and Alperowitz, 2002).

But local dependence extends well beyond capitals that are relatively fixed. Most of the institutions that help to form a "common sense"—schools, newspapers (with a few national exceptions like *USA Today*), places of worship, and local governments—are, for all intents and purposes, place dependent. Also, for longtime residents of a place, mobility often does not seem like an option given the variety and intensity of the social relationships and networks the residents have often constructed. These residents are functionally just as place dependent as any fixed investment. Together, these are the actors that engage in local political struggles, not just over economic development but over the entire spectrum of political conflict, ranging from school district battles to housing and commercial-zoning disputes.

When these arguments are brought together, we can arrive at a working definition of localities. The locality can be understood as: the scale of experience, constructed through power relations and conflicts between those social actors and structures that are functionally immobile as they try to create a "common sense" and define their position in their relations with the supralocal world. Localities, therefore are never fixed entities. At the same time, however, many of the relationships that those within a locality are engaged in are relatively stable and can be viewed as "permanences"

(Harvey, 1996). We must therefore be careful not to construct a view of localities that is too process-based and fluid to be intellectually and political useful. These permanences are not themselves neutral in any sense, but instead are the stabilization of the outcomes of the conflicts and relationships that produce localities. An archetypal example of these permanences can be found in the boundaries that separate political jurisdictions—cities from suburbs—in American metropolitan areas. Often viewed as fixed or arbitrary lines in interconnected urban areas, these boundaries are instead the geographic codification of power relations and political struggles over the production and definition of localities. These boundaries were usually the results of upper-income whites working to disassociate themselves, and their property taxes, from inner-city residents. Once codified, these boundaries, in turn, act to produce the conditions for social and political life within metropolitan areas—through such mechanisms as local school-district allocations—and work to reproduce the wealth of the people who are on "the right side" of the boundaries. Localities, through their permanences, therefore act as "emergent forms" that greatly enable or constrain the possible future actions of people and institutions within them. The questions therefore become: How are the relations that produce localities stabilized (or codified)? Who decides? With what logic and values? And at what geographic scale are those decisions made? These are, or at least should be, the core questions of local and community politics.

Local Autonomy

The idea of autonomy has a long history in western thought connected with the individual's ability to act in a liberal democracy, and has been understood as something held by people (or not held) as they entered the public arena to participate in democracy. At the heart of this traditional view of autonomy is the understanding that possessing autonomy means having the ability to act without outside interference or constraints. That is, autonomy, in this usage, is the freedom (and autonomy is a close sibling to "freedom" in liberal democratic thought) to act independently of, and almost in isolation from, the outside world.

Attempts to theorize local autonomy by Saunders (1979), Clark (1984), Gurr and King (1987), and Wolman and Goldsmith (1990, 1992; Goldsmith, 1995) do so with many of these same understandings. There are, however, fundamental problems with these conceptions. First, they treat autonomy as something that is either possessed or not possessed by localities as they enter the policy-making process. But autonomy is a form and expression of power and, as such, it is not a static thing granted or possessed by individuals, states, or localities (and localities, as argued above, cannot *possess* anything, since they do not, in a strict sense, exist as agents or actors). Instead autonomy is a relational construct. Second, in these conceptions of autonomy, autonomy is a function of the locality's ability to act independently of outside forces or in isolation from outside influence or constraints. But if we have defined localities as partly a function of the extralocal social relationships they are embedded within, then clearly our conception of local autonomy cannot require the isolation of localities.

Since autonomy is a form of power, any theoretical understanding of it must emerge from an understanding of power. As Brown (1992, p. 263) put it, "Power is not what a social object 'holds'; it is how that object is linked to other social objects in enabling or constraining ways." Foucault further argued that power relations are constitutive of all social interactions, and cannot be rooted solely in any class, social group, or institution. At the same time, however, he recognized that institutions become foci for the exercise of power. Therefore, while power relations are all-pervasive, they are not without specific forms or divorced from social structures and institutions. For instance, if President Bush were to be marooned on a desert island, he would certainly cease to be a powerful person. He obviously does not "possess" power. He is powerful because of the formal and informal institutional, structural, and personal relationships that produce "the president."

Similar arguments were made by Poulantzas (1978) and Jessop (1990) in their discussions of the state. They argue that the state is a social relation, and that state power is therefore the codification of power relations. As such, this codification process is not a neutral one, and the emergent institutions are themselves immersed in the complex web of power relations. The power relations that are codified into the institutions, logically, therefore continue to express themselves in and through those institutions. The result is that different political projects and goals operate with different sets of barriers and opportunities. There is, in short, a "Structural Selectivity" (Poulantzas, 1978) in how the state operates, which yields a very uneven political playing field.

So what does all this mean for an understanding of local autonomy? First, it means that we need to understand autonomy as a form of power and that autonomy is therefore a relational construct. Autonomy is not a *thing* but a process and a set of complexrelationships. For local-scale actors to be autonomous, they must therefore transform the relations they are embedded in to allow themselves greater control over those relationships. Second, autonomy might be relational, but that does not make it amorphous, unidentifiable, or placeless. And autonomy might not exist in itself, but it does find expression in the institutions that lie at the focal points of a locality's relations. When Lake (1994) defines local autonomy as, "the capacity of localities to control the social construction of place," he is really talking about the ability of local-scale actors to control the institutions that connect them to the rest of the world. Third, the possibility of local auton-omy is partially a function of the political goals of those trying to realize it. The current set of power relations in the capitalist political economy, and the hegemony of capital that is both an outcome of those power relations and constitutive of them, means that local-scale projects confront different opportunity structures as they attempt to gain control over their relations with the extralocal world. For local-scale political projects antithetical to capital, the possibilities of realizing autonomy are significantly con-strained, and Conroy's (1990) excellent case study of the institutional bar-riers faced by the Socialists in local government in Burlington, Vermont, provides a powerful reminder of this.

None of this is to say, however, that place-based actors could ever com-pletely control the production of their locality, or realize complete auton-omy in their relations with the rest of the world, regardless of the political projects undertaken or the institutional framework constructed. Localities are too embedded in, and constructed through, too many social relation-ships for those within them to ever fully control how they are produced. Also, autonomy, like all forms of power, is inherently met by opposition, and the conflicts over the production of a locality are never fully resolved, only periodically made less explicit in the form of permanences. Local au-tonomy, therefore, can be defined as the ever-contested and never com-plete ability of those within the locality to control the institutions and relationships that define and produce the locality.

With this definition of local autonomy, an understanding of the NUP becomes possible. Both conclusions (no autonomy and hyper-autonomy) are too simplistic. The increased mobility of capital has not rendered local-ities powerless (or "taken" away localities' autonomy). Localities have al-ways been produced through a complex set of relations with the extralocal world. The current mobility of capital simply means that, in order for agents within localities to realize autonomy, they must construct struc-tures and institutions of capital accumulation that limit the potential for mobility by transforming the scale at which capital is dependent.

Conversely, the increased possibility to attract newly mobile capital has not generated any form of hyper-local autonomy because the production of the localities is still controlled by larger-scale capital. That is, the ability to define places as simply sites of capital accumulation remains uncon-tested if autonomy is understood as the ability to make conditions right for the attraction of outside capital investment. Using Lefebvre's framework, in the New Localist school, control over the representations of space (how it is conceived, invested in, and constructed) remains with larger-scale cap-ital, and not with local-scale actors. Until the relational and processual qualities of locality and autonomy are understood, the debates of the NUP will continue to be misguided theoretical projects that lead local politics toward inadequately narrow and constrained set of policy choices.

The Politics of the New Urban Politics and Its Alternatives

Finally, an important point about the political implications of the framework of the debates of the NUP, which I've hinted at, needs to be made explicit. The assumption that capital mobility and economic globalization exist and operate as a "done deal" is a devastating political outcome of these public policy and academic debates. And it has furthered the political and economic inequalities I described earlier. Either way, if localities genuinely are able to attract mobile capital or are powerless to do anything in the face of that capital, they are still left with no real options. A reasonable person could ask if it is better for a local government to "give away the store" to attract a business—and therefore gain little from its presence—or not do so, and continue to struggle with a lack of employment for its residents? Simply put, if capital mobility is accepted as a given, then the entire framework for local action has been determined by capital, and in ways that are very profitable to capital. David Harvey makes this point rather forcefully:

> There is a strong predilection these days to regard the future of urbanization as already determined by the powers of globalization and of market competition. Urban possibilities are limited to mere competitive jockeying of individual cities for position within the urbanization process from which to launch any kind of militant particularism capable of grounding the drive for systemic transformation . . . The ideological effect of this discursive shift has been extraordinarily disempowering with respect to all forms of local, urban, and even national political action (Harvey, 1996, p. 420).

A quick example from the economic development policies of the NUP should clarify the political implications of assuming capital mobility. As already discussed, city governments have become increasingly willing to invest public money in economic development projects. These public investments, however, have had the effect of liberating capital from places. This is because the risks associated with investment, and therefore the losses associated with disinvestment, are now absorbed by municipal governments, and not capital itself. If a business does not invest its own money into a project in a place, what would prevent it from leaving? City governments, therefore, in their efforts to attract mobile capital, have furthered the processes of capital mobility. They have, in short, enabled a self-fulfilling prophecy. It is exactly this point that Piven was making in the quote that began this chapter. One of the primary goals of this whole project, therefore, is to explore the possibilities for local autonomy that might exist outside the frameworks given above. For it is only outside those frameworks that local autonomy might be realized in ways that equitably improve the conditions under which we all live and work.

But there is, of course, a potential contradiction in the reasoning just presented. That is, it posits the goal of local autonomy at the same time as the goal of social justice and equity in American cities. But why should we assume that local control is going to mean a diminution of unequal and unjust power relations? If we take Foucault seriously, then we must recognize that power relations within the scale of the locality might be just as oppressive as those between a locality and the supralocal world. As Sennett, in response to the community control movement of the early 1970s (see chapter 2 of this volume), argued, "Localism and local autonomy are becoming widespread political creeds, as though the experiences of power relations will have more human meaning the more intimate the scale" (Sennett, 1977, p. 339). This point is well-taken, and it was the recognized oppression that existed *within* cities, and not between cities and the larger world, that led to the community control movement in the first place. Also, not only can localities and communities oppress certain groups and individuals within them, but they can also construct themselves in exclusionary ways. In fact, the localities that come closest to realizing local autonomy might be the white rural militia communities in Montana (and elsewhere), or the ex-urban gated communities that dot the landscape in Orange County, California (and elsewhere). Given their inherently exclusionary nature (whether such exclusion is based on race or class or both), these are clearly not the models to which we should be looking.

But these arguments notwithstanding, autonomy has to be a goal for low-income communities struggling against disinvestment they can't control and which robs them of decent affordable housing and stable employment, or, conversely, reinvestment from without which comes in the form of displacement, gentrification, and the war against the poor. The reality is that people in low-income neighborhoods, almost by definition, lack the capital or political strength to act individually to realize their goals. Individuals, of course, can, and do, succeed in realizing personal financial security, but the problem is that doing so is often accompanied by—or requires—leaving the low-income neighborhood. Therefore we are returned to forms of collective action, collective ownership, and *collective control* which, theoretically, limit the potential for structured inequities and oppressions.

Beyond the Theory: Finding Autonomous and Equitable Development in Practice

As suggested above, the vast majority of city governments and, as will be discussed in chapter 2, community-based organizations, have responded to the current mobility of capital by embracing the NUP, and creating conditions deemed appropriate to attracting capital. At the same time, however, alternative forms of development have been constructed that are organized around the goal of "reclaiming" that capital by limiting its potential mobility by "anchoring" it within localities (Bruyn and Meehan, 1987; Douthwaite, 1996; Gunn and Gunn, 1991; Imbroscio, 1997; Shavelson, 1990; Shuman, 1998; Wilkenson and Quarter, 1996; Williamson, Imbroscio, Alperowitz, 2002). This has been done in a variety of ways, including locally based ownership of work (in worker and community organization cooperatives, and ESOPs), home (in limited-equity cooperatives, Community Land Trusts, and Mutual Housing Associations), and money (by controlling credit through community development credit unions and local exchange trading systems). At the heart of all of these strategies is the creation of institutions of capital accumulation that are locally owned and controlled. Since localities are not agents, however, they cannot *own* anything. Instead, forms of local ownership are created by collective ownership or ownership by organizations or institutions that are place bound (or place dependent). This is fundamentally different from creating forms of ownership for individuals who happen to reside within localities. While individual owners may die, retire, or relocate, collectives and organizations are much less likely to do so (although they may certainly fail). Also, given the diversity that exists within any locality, forms of collective ownership in which control is relatively decentralized, offer a much greater potential for *local*, rather than individual, autonomy. These forms of collective ownership insure greater local control over the processes of investment and disinvestment, and therefore offer the potential for greater control over the production of the locality. This chapter will only briefly introduce these institutions, as they will be discussed in much greater length in chapters three through five.

While worker-owned cooperatives have long been a part of the American industrial landscape, they began to take on new meaning in the 1970s and 1980s as plant closings and relocations became commonplace in the economic geography of the older industrial regions in this country. Worker-ownership has been transformed, therefore, from an issue of workplace relations and the market for equity shares, to one which has foregrounded community economic development (Olson, 1987; Megson and O'Toole, 1993; Wilkenson and Quarter, 1996; Wills, 1998).[4] Threatened plant closures have been met by attempts by union locals and/or communities to buy the condemned factories. Even when the community is relatively uninvolved, employee-ownership can serve to maintain the importance of place in the decision-making process. Workers, as a collective, are simply more place dependent than the business might otherwise be.

Collective ownership of housing can take several forms. Most common is the limited-equity housing cooperative. In a limited-equity co-op, the residents own the units collectively but, in order to insure the long-term affordability of the housing, their ability to profit from their ownership is greatly constrained. Similarly in a community land trust, a community organization owns and manages the land, while the residents "own" only the housing units located on the land. This community ownership is structured to protect the long-term affordability of the housing units in trust, and to insure that the community is in control of decisions made about the investment or disinvestment in the housing stock within the community. Mutual Housing Associations (MHAs) are similar to both limited-equity co-ops and CLTs, but in this institutional arrangement the community organization directly owns the housing units as well as the land, and the residents have no equity investment in their housing.

There are currently between 300 and 400 community development credit unions (CDCUs) in the United States (National Federation of Community Development Credit Unions, 1998), and their primary goal is to bring basic banking services to communities where the market is not providing those services. Like all credit unions, they are member-owned cooperatives that require a recognized commonality among members. But unlike the majority of credit unions, they are organized in low-income communities, often centered around a church-based organization, and the CDCUs are explicitly created to promote local economic development. Local exchange trading systems (LETS) are forms of exchange based on reciprocity within a community—with the reciprocal relationship formalized in the form of local currencies.

None of these forms of local economic development seeks autonomy through cutting off the locality's relationships with the rest of the world. All of these institutions are very much *inside* the capitalist political economy. Plant closings and credit-union failures are all very real occurrences and are testaments to their existence as part of capitalism (Deasy, 1998; Gunn, 1992; Wilkenson and Quarter, 1996). Control over the decisions made within that economy, however, is fundamentally altered. The "logic of the market," which is usually, if inaccurately, understood to be placeless and noncorporeal, is transformed by locally based organizations at the nexus of control over investment and disinvestment. Collective ownership therefore transforms the codification of the power relations that constitute investment decisions. The market is not rejected but the power relations that constitute "the market" are restructured. In so doing, collective ownership alters the scale of ownership and renders capital place dependent when it otherwise would not be.

But the possibility of local autonomy is greater than just the control over capital investment sought by organizations creating these forms of collective ownership. By having worker-, resident-, or member-control structured into their governance, and by often claiming their identity as spatially embedded in the *place* of the community, these organizations are part of the process of creating those communities. As these place-dependent collectives have organized around local economic development, they have transformed the "common sense" that, in turn, partially constructs and defines the localities.

This logic, however, can be taken one step farther. If these alternative practices allow for locally controlled meanings to be constructed, they offer the potential for those meanings to not simply be alternative but to be counterhegemonic. This is, admittedly, asking a lot from these local practices. Hegemony is not simply a function of being in a position of power in social relationships and conflicts, but is rather the ability to define the terms of struggles in the first place. This is not simply the Marxist axiom that the ideology of the ruling class becomes the dominant ideology of society, but that the dominant ideology is able to infiltrate the meanings attributed to the routine practices which constitute everyday life. Hegemonic power is therefore as productive as it is constraining and oppressive. Hegemonic ideologies are also not static and immutable but open to contestation and malleable, able to absorb practices that might initially appear to be antithetical. It is thus a tall order to expect these organizations to be counterhegemonic.

This is where the potential for the realization of local autonomy can truly be found: in local economic development organizations that have recognized the relationships and institutions that connect their locality with the rest of the world, have enacted institutional change to increase their control over those relationships, and have created *new localities and new social meanings* in the process.

Concluding Remarks

This, therefore, is the theory behind this project: That collective ownership, either directly by workers or residents, or indirectly via a community organization, will be able to transform the relations that produce the locality, and do so in ways that improve the quality of life for those involved. Capital mobility and economic restructuring have created a context in which localities seemingly have fewer options on the table than before. The empirical question of this project is whether or not these forms of collective ownership really do engender local autonomy. And, in short, is the field of possible local action limited to the dichotomies of the new localists and city-limits arguments. Or is it large enough to allow for forms of ownership that might directly challenge capital mobility and globalization?

CHAPTER **2**

Collective Ownership
and Community Control
and Development
The Long View

The left in the United States suffers from a peculiar historical amnesia.
Few free-school founders or food co-op enthusiasts in the sixties learned anything
from their predecessors in previous decades, because they had never heard of them.
The lessons of the recent past are just as obscure to the scattered activists of
the present. New arrangements for living and working persist, but often in a vacuum.
—John Case and Rosemary Taylor, 1979

There is very little new about the solutions proposed in chapter 1 except the context in which they emerged. People in the United States have been creating forms of collective ownership and working toward the goal of local or community control for a long time. In order not to lose sight of the lessons of these histories, we need to explore them here. The histories of collective ownership, community development, and local/community control are varied and disparate, and it is the rather ambitious goal of this chapter to bring these histories together. For while these organizations, and, at times, movements, emerged at different times and in different places for different reasons, there are substantial relationships among them. Equally important, however, are the disjunctures that have existed, and which continue to exist. Beginning with the nineteenth-century American roots of collective ownership and community control, the chapter then shifts to the 1960s and discusses the emergence of the current community-development movement. It then presents the trajectory of this movement away from its organizing roots and toward greater degrees of institutionalization and professionalization. This professionalization has seen the goal of community control, and the radical politics that sometimes informed that goal, get lost in the process. The chapter concludes by discussing the implications of this history.

Co-ops, Communes, Collectives, and Community Control in American History

Nineteenth-Century Black Communes

The history of community control in the United States has several different components, but in terms of providing the roots for the emergence of community ownership, the most important of these is the history of black "organized communities" of the nineteenth century. These communities were created primarily in the Northwest of the United States (Michigan, Indiana, Ohio, and Wisconsin) and in Southern Ontario in Canada (Pease and Pease, 1963). The goals of these organizations were to provide sites of isolation and independence from the racism of white North America, and to create a context in which individual blacks could prosper and learn to live freely. In short, "they saw in a community organization the possibility of presenting a common front to a hostile environment, and in common effort they recognized the virtue of mutual aid and assistance and the pooling of resources until such a time as the individual Negro settler could manage on his own" (Pease and Pease, 1963, pp. 16–17). As the above quote suggests, the goal of these communes, unlike their nonblack contemporaries, was not to construct forms of local socialism or communism but instead was unapologetically capitalist and individualist in purposes and organizing principles. They believed in the dominant Victorian ideals of self-help and individualism, and the goals of these communes were to train blacks to fit into what they perceived as the emergent American middle class. At the same time, the American ideal was also still enmeshed in Jefferson's vision of an agrarian populace and in a skepticism of the still barely emerging urban industrial class. So the goals of these communes were to turn freed slaves into Gentleman Farmers, and priority was given to working the soil as a means for improving the character of the individual freed slaves (although it is not clear why this would improve the character of those involved since they had come from situations where, as slaves, very often all they did was work the soil!). Started in the 1830s, these communes disappeared shortly after the end of the Civil War (with the passage of the Thirteenth Amendment to the Constitution), and their impacts on American society were largely negligible. In their assessment, Pease and Pease conclude, "what is most impressive of all about this adventure in humane salvation and massive uplift is the fact that the results were, on the whole, so trag-ically inconsequential" (Pease and Pease, 1963, p. 160).

These communes essentially prefigured the beliefs that Booker T. Wash-ington disseminated during the Reconstruction Era about blacks needing to succeed in business in order to interact with whites on an equal footing. Washington continued the arguments of the communes by arguing that this equality could be realized by blacks only if they isolated themselves in order for blacks to enter into positions of authority, and then, from those segregated positions of authority, blacks could engage with whites in com-parable positions (Washington, 1971). Washington, accordingly, was not an integrationist and he argued: "Let us in the future spend less time talk-ing about the part of the city that we cannot live in, and more time making the part of the city that we live in beautiful and attractive" (quoted in Philpot, 1978, p. 209). Washington was also an unmitigated believer in the potential of capitalism to allow blacks to realize class mobility (although his capitalism was shaped by the industrial world that had developed in the time between the 1830s and his post–Civil War writing), and so he cease-lessly advocated that blacks develop industrial trade schools and become tradesmen. He stated:

> More and more thoughtful students of the race problem are beginning to see that business and industry constitute what we may call the strategic point in its solution. These fundamental professions we are able to occupy not only with-out resistance but even with encouragement, and from them we shall gradually advance to all the rights and privileges which any class of citizens enjoy (Wash-ington, 1971, p. 19).

The invisibility of class structure and class conflict in his analysis is nothing short of astonishing. As we will see, Washington's arguments, in turn, provided much of the foundation for the emergence of the black cap-italism and community economic-development movement of the 1960s (Halpern, 1995; Hampden-Turner, 1975; Perry, 1972).

Co-ops, Communes, and Utopian Socialists

While the black communes emerged in the 1830s and were explicitly geared toward reproducing agrarian and mercantile capitalism in black communities, there was a parallel and yet completely different history of nineteenth-century communes and collectives that were oriented toward exactly the opposite goal—creating places outside the constraints and structures of the emergent industrial capitalist world of wage slavery and employment-based production. These "utopian" communities were at-tempts at local-scale communism, and they were largely divided between secular and religious communes, although there was a good deal of overlap (Nordhoff, 1993).

While the religious communes were larger in number than the secular ones, the secular communes, based on the goals of creating localized socialist communes, are the more relevant to us here. These nineteenth-century experiments with communism were ideologically a combination of Jeffersonian agrarian democracy (and his acceptance of Locke's labor theory of property) and British socialism. The work of the British socialist Robert Owen was particularly important to the creation of these communes, and he moved to the United States in 1825 to implement his ideas (Curl, 1980). Various forms of these communes grew in rural areas until shortly before the Civil War, and it has been argued that these communist experiments had a substantial impact on the young Frederich Engels in the mid 1840s (see Feuer, 1966). But they foundered in the 1850s, as greater numbers of Americans became workers in the emerging industrial economy, and the communes were unable to reach them (Curl, 1980). Efforts were made to renew this form of localized, independent communism in the 1880s and 1890s, but by then the model had been disparaged by Marx and Engels as not only unable to transform society, but also reactionary (in the sense of backward-looking). The political energy needed to resurrect it therefore proved too much to muster. In the end, these isolated, localized communes had little impact on the burgeoning industrial capitalist country of the nineteenth-century. As Oved (1988, pp. 14–15) argues, "The commune never became an integral part of the forces that formed the nation . . . Even when they flourished, the commune and its revolutionary lifestyle never endangered the trend of American society. Communes remained a marginal factor, and this . . . is perhaps the reason why there was no attempt to undermine or uproot them." Thus the nineteenth-century communes—black or white, religious or secular—had little impact on the larger world around them mostly due to their goal of opting out, although the reasons differed. This lesson should have been learned by those who created the 1960s incarnations of the commune, were it not for the amnesia cited at the beginning of this chapter.

Things Come Together, Things Fall Apart: The Experience of the 1960s

These two traditions of very different kinds of communes and co-ops converged for a brief period in the mid- to late 1960s, but the convergence was short-lived, constituted by and constitutive of several other social movements. Community (or neighborhood) control reemerged as a broad set of movements in this period, but their strands remained distinct—in their goals, ideological justifications, and institutional forms. Broadly speaking, there were three different strands to this movement—the black power movement, the direct democracy movement, and the cooperative living movement—but they often overlapped, and each strand was itself not unitary but consisted of multiple components. This convergence yielded many institutional and structural innovations and changes (some short-lived, others much more durable) but for the purposes of this project, the most important institution to emerge was the "community development corporation" (CDC), which was, and is, the principle institutional vehicle for community development in the United States. But before we discuss the emergent social-movement from which sprang community development, as a programmatic idea, and the CDC, its vehicle, we need to discuss the context of American politics that both fostered these movements and severely undercut their ability to effect systematic change.

From CAAs to Model Cities and Beyond

The federal government enacted the Economic Opportunity Act in 1964 and with it, began the well-known period of the "War on Poverty." While this war on poverty contained a diverse set of institutions, for the purposes of this discussion, the most important components of this legislation were its creation of the Office of Economic Opportunity (OEO), and a new vehicle for community-based organizing, planning, and activism, the "community action agency" (CAA). The heart of the CAA initiative was community empowerment and activism, and the underlying philosophy of the Community Action Program (CAP, which was responsible for overseeing the CAAs) was the "maximum feasible participation" of community members—particularly low-income blacks. This drive in federal policy was a complete change from its earlier practice of ignoring local communities during the early Urban Renewal programs of the 1950s. It probably, however, reflected the needs of the Democratic party to generate black involvement in formal politics as much as it was a response to the increasing demands for power by the civil-rights movement which had moved north during the late 1950s and early 1960s (Fisher, 1994).

It is unclear, at best, if within three years the CAAs were able to generate substantial community-level mobilization efforts—and this varied from city to city. In many cities, they simply became service delivery "watchdogs" whose radical potential was rather limited, while in many of the more organized and mobilized cities, the conflictual nature of the CAAs meant that it was "all conflict, all the time." And by 1967, "they were sufficiently threatening or persuasive to precipitate a ange in] national urban policy" (Fainstein, 1987, p. 328). This shift in policy had two particular components. First, the CAAs were to be reoriented toward economic development activities, and away from the much more broadly understood political organizing goals of their initial inception. The legislative form this shift in priorities took was that of the passage of the Special Impact Program (SIP) amendment to the OEO, which was written by Senator Robert Kennedy after his famous visit to Bedford-Stuyvesant, Brooklyn, in 1966 (Peirce and Steinbach, 1987). The SIP legislation targeted local groups for specifically economic development projects, and this program was supplemented by the Federal Community Self-Determination Act in 1969, which drove the creation of many Community Development Corporations. Although the first CDCs had actually been created somewhat earlier in 1967, and in several different cities, it was after SIP and the 1969 Self-Determination Act that they really started to grow. And this growth was accomplished because of substantial amounts of federal support (Perry, 1971).

The second component of the shift in federal policies was the enactment of the Model Cities Program, designed to place the control over antipoverty/neighborhood development policies back into the hands of city governments—and explicitly away from the hands of communities. As Halpern puts it: "Model Cities was to be community development decoupled from community action, or more specifically from community action's presumed tendency to engender conflict and disaffection" (Halpern, 1995, p. 118). This shift indicated how threatened many city governments were by the CAP. By funding CAAs directly, the OEO and CAP were enabling community organizations to bypass city governments and connect directly to national politics and priorities. Community groups had therefore been able to jump scales, while city governments were unable to do so.

These shifts in federal policies had profound implications for the practice of community organizing at the time. Groups had to choose between becoming more professionalized development organizations or maintain their political identity. But maintaining their political identity would mean the loss of the federal and, after the Model Cities Program, local funding they had come to rely on. Either way, the potential and capacity for radical community organizing and social change was significantly undercut. As Kotler observed shortly thereafter, "The government wanted enterprise rather than political action in the neighborhood; it would move the people out of the meeting hall and put them behind cash registers" (Kotler, 1971, p. 7).

To some extent, therefore, 1960s' federal neighborhood policy represented a very narrow window through which connections between community-level political organizing and community-based economic development and social service provision could be merged. But that window closed rather quickly and, in doing so, helped to solidify the divisions between organizing and development, which have come to be a dominant feature in urban politics in the last quarter century.

Black Power and Black Capitalism

While the federal government was both supporting and limiting the opportunities for community empowerment in the 1960s, one of the most powerful forces in driving issues of community control was the emergent "black power" movement, a product of the civil-rights movement, which had been mobilizing since at least the early 1950s. A significant strand of the black-power movement was the drive for "community control" (Altshuler, 1970; Carmichael and Hamilton, 1967). The movement for "community control," which was race-based, had two distinct components. First it dealt specifically with issues of government decentralization and black participation and control. This was particularly true for issues of education and policing. Second, it addressed the control over economic relations between blacks and whites. While the former segment represented a substantial set of issues and conflicts in American cities (see Fainstein and Fainstein, 1976, for a discussion of these), the latter of these two helped drive the creation of the CDC and also foreshadowed the central issue of this project: Can people acting in their communities control the economic relationships that connect them to the rest of the world?

There was not a clear, unifying underlying rationale of the economic component of the community control movement, and instead there was a variety of programs, goals, and ideals. This, of course, echoed the long-standing debates by black leaders about how to structure, organize, and promote black economic development. The 1960s' version of this argument was made from a variety of different positions, ranging from direct community ownership by CDCs in black neighborhoods, to co-operative ownership by blacks, to individually owned forms of capital accumulation by blacks. Despite the debates about what form black ownership should take, some of its most visible proponents were decidedly ambivalent about it. Roy Innis, the director of the Congress of Racial Equality (CORE), was one of the principal proponents of black ownership, and his arguments, which exemplify the incoherence of this ambivalence, deserve to be quoted at length here. He stated:

> In the new focus on economic control, there has been much talk about something called 'black capitalism' . . . There is no such animal. Capitalism, like socialism, is an economic and political philosophy that describes the experience of Europeans and their descendants—Americans. Blacks must innovate, must create a new ideology. It may include elements of capitalism, elements of socialism, or elements of neither: *That is immaterial.* What matters is that it will be created to fit our needs (Innis, 1969, pp. 52–53, emphasis added).

This ambivalence led, fairly quickly, to a reassertion of Booker T. Washington's Reconstruction Era arguments about the central role of black entrepreneurialism and capitalism in the realization of power within the black community. So despite powerful criticisms of black capitalism (see Boggs, 1970; Kain and Persky, 1971; Sturdivant, 1969) it became, through its promotion by OEO policies, the Nixon administration, and the lack of clarity about issues of ownership by leaders in black communities, the dominant form of black economic "community" control by the end of the 1960s. It should also be noted that the Community Self-Determination Act was co-authored by CORE and the Nixon presidential campaign, and the politics surrounding its passage were a peculiar combination of black power advocates and Rockefeller Republicans (see McClaughry, 1969). As Harold Cruse perceptively noted at the time, this segment of the black power movement, "is *nothing but the economic and political philosophy of Booker T. Washington given a 1960s militant shot in the arm and brought up to date*" (Cruse, 1969, p. 114, emphasis in original). Community control, in its economic guise, remarkably quickly became an argument in support of black capitalism, and advocates for both consciously and unconsciously conflated these two goals (Allen, 1969; Faux, 1971; Green and Faux, 1969; McKersie, 1968; Perry, 1972; Sclar, 1970). The radical potential of demands for black economic power thus became co-opted and transformed into simply a debate about how best to reproduce capitalist practices in black urban neighborhoods. The road of collective *community* control and empowerment was not taken (Shipp, 1996). A substantial political opportunity was lost.

Direct Democracy and Neighborhood Government

While the community control argument was being presented by black-power activists and theorists, a nominally comparable but substantively different argument was being presented by those advocating neighborhood control and neighborhood government. These activists and writers were advocating government decentralization as a means to politically empowering the citizens of urban areas. In short, this movement represented another incarnation of the Jeffersonian liberal traditional of populism and small-scale participatory government. As Wilson put it, "It is primarily at the neighborhood level that meaningful [i.e., potentially rewarding] opportunities for the exercise of urban citizenship exist" (Wilson, 1968, p. 28). Jane Jacobs similarly wrote from Toronto, "The governments of large modern cities are not only incomprehensibly complex today, but also their direct effects on citizen's lives are now so ubiquitous that they cannot help but fail when their functions are centrally organized. Many functions must be decentralized and brought under direct, continuing control of local communities" (quoted in Repo, 1977, p. 48).

But perhaps the strongest supporter of the neighborhood democracy movement was Milton Kotler, who would eventually become the executive director of the National Association of Neighborhoods. He was clear about what he saw as, "the radical politics of local control" (Kotler, 1969), as a rejection of both the centralized welfare policies of the New Deal/Great Society variety, and the central role of class in leftist politics. Both of these should be replaced, he argued, by an embrace of the Ancient Greek view of humans as almost inherently political beings mixed with a twentieth-century perspective on the declining ability of humans to act as such (see Arendt, 1958). He argued that "True radicalism issues from a practical view of man's political nature, rather than a theoretical view of the state. Its object is to shape the state to fit the present purpose of popular struggle—local rule—not to reshape man to fit a theoretical state. For the left to engage in a politics of liberty requires that it free itself of the modern heritage of revolution and address the principles of local control" (Kotler, 1969, p. 96). Thus, like the black community control movement, when push came to shove, not only did the neighborhood government movement fail to address issues of capital and class relations, it actually embraced the capitalist political economy, albeit with a rejection of its bureaucratized and centralized Keynesian form.

This was, in short, a movement for localized democracy as an end in itself, not a movement to use the framework of local democracy for changes in larger-scale, *or even local*, economic structures and relations. The movement for neighborhood control was not without its political victories and, together with the state-centered wing of the black community control movement, it did affect some institutional changes, most notably in the creation of Boston's "Little City Halls," and New York City's (now defunct) school districts and Community Boards (Fainstein and Fainstein, 1976). But even these institutional victories did not mark a substantial wresting of control from municipal governments by neighborhoods (Marcuse, 1987).

Co-ops, Communes, and Collectives

At the same time that the efforts for black power and direct democracy were being undertaken, the history of communal and collective ownership entered a new phase. During the 1960s, various forms of collective ownership were being created. These efforts tended to be small in scale and very localized in their goals and orientations. Also, the collectives tended to be centered around the institutions of social-service provision and social reproduction: Free schools, communal housing and, consumer co-operatives were the primary forms of this re-emergence. The goals of these forms of collectives ranged from the fairly apolitical cooperatives (see Dodge, 1964) to "counterinstitutions" of the New Left. Adherents of the latter wanted to construct a new society, and took seriously Mao's story of the old man who shocked his neighbors by moving a mountain one stone at a time as a parable of how small changes can have a cumulative impact on society. They wanted, in short, to "live the revolution" (Moberg, 1979).

At the same time, this was largely a movement of disaffected middle-class white Americans, and was not predicated on a complex analysis of class or race structures. The co-ops', and communes', small size (often no bigger than a communal house in a city) belied their criticisms of the larger society and their conscious goal of using the new institutions as a model to transform that society. Alternative (i.e., collectively owned and controlled) institutions were created throughout the country, but despite their political content, these counterinstitutions were only loosely connected to the larger political movements of the time. This was partly a function of their limited size but also a result of how they constructed themselves in the form of communes. Communes tend to be separatist and closed, which does not easily translate into connected components of a larger movement. In her analysis of American communes, Cavan (1976) found these two attributes (along with the voluntary involvement of their members) to be what characterize communes in the first place, and what distinguishes them from other small-scale social networks and subsocieties. All of this resulted in the demise of most of the communes in the 1970s, and many of the education and social-service reforms initiated became parts of the larger bureaucratic structures that these groups emerged as an "alternative" to in the first place. The echoes of the nineteenth-century communes' experiences were striking. Both were unable to substantially transform society because change cannot be affected by simply "opting out," but instead requires direct confrontations with the structures that govern the political economy. This is an issue that we will return to later in this project.

Opportunities Lost

The possibilities of connecting these three separate movements, all struggling for local control, albeit in somewhat different forms, were always fairly slim. And in many basic ways, they were fighting for different goals and had very different constituencies. But, at the same time, they were conscious political efforts to create institutions in which local-scale actors had greater control over their lives. They also shared a rhetorical belief in "community" participation and control. Participatory democracy was, stated or unstated, a central goal of these groups, and it was this goal that brought these activists together, on paper at least in the form of books written at the time (see, in particular, Benello and Roussopoulos, 1971).

At the same time, their understandings of capital and class were extremely limited and none of these forms of local control directly confronted capital or even adequately theorized capitalism. In this way, the movements failed to appreciate the inherent importance of capital and class relations in structuring the American political economy. As Ira Katnelson (1981) argues in his exceptional book, this failure to understand class leads to movements sliding into the prefigured "trenches" of American urban politics in which *class* is dealt with at work, and *community* is dealt with at home—and both are dealt with inadequately. And in sliding into those trenches, the invisibility of class in American public life is reproduced. This set the community and neighborhood control efforts up to either disappear or become institutionally co-opted. And this is largely what happened in the 1970s and 1980s.

From Community Control to Community-Based Development: 1970 to the Present

The period that stretches from the early 1970s to the present has often been described as one in which there is a general decline in the levels of local-scale political organizing, or the "death of urban politics" referred to in chapter 1. While there is certainly a degree of truth to this statement, it is also an oversimplification of local and community politics. Instead, this period can better be described as one in which there has been an increasing disassociation of explicitly political community organizing from community development. Both continue, but they are too often conflated, with the latter being assumed to stand for the former. As such, CDCs are no longer seen as vehicles for community control but instead are characterized as sources for "community-based" activities like housing or "development." This divide, which began in the 1960s with the changing funding priorities of the OEO splitting CDCs from CAAs, is reproduced and strengthened with each generation of community development and organizing groups. But I am getting ahead of myself, and I must first discuss the trends in community or, more appropriate to the time, neighborhood organizing in the 1970s.

Neo-Alinskyism and the Neighborhood Movements of the 1970s

Often described as distinct from what had come in the preceding decade, local politics in the 1970s is better understood as having evolved from the earlier period, particularly from the direct democracy strand of organizing. Local politics were dominated in this decade by what has been called "the neighborhood movement" (*Social Policy*, 1979). In truth, this was less a movement than a diverse set of localized responses to particular issues that largely stemmed from people's attempts to protect their neighborhoods from threats and encroachments from without. Accordingly, the politics of the organizations in this "movement" varied tremendously, largely in relation to the character of the threat from without and the perceived sources of that threat.

As this "Backyard Revolution" (Boyte, 1980) was taking place, a set of populist organizations emerged that were large in scale (often state- or nation-wide) and relatively unencumbered by an ideologically defined set of goals. The principal intellectual figure in this movement was Saul Alinsky who, although he had been organizing in Chicago since before World War II, had emerged nationally as a prominent critic of the explicitly socialist and race-based organizing efforts of the 1960s. Instead, he and his organization, the Industrial Areas Foundation (IAF), argued for a brand of organizing that assumed that the only long-term goal should be the mobilization of people to take power for themselves. After working for the Congress of Industrial Organizations (CIO) in the late 1930s, he argued that working-class political organizing needed to be free of the ideological framework of class, and that:

> It is not just trying to deal with the factory manager, but with every element and aspect, whether it be political, economical or social that makes up the life of the worker . . . so that instead of viewing itself as a separate section of the American people engaged in a separate craft in a particular industry, it will think of itself as an organization of *American citizens* (Alinsky, 1969, p. 36, emphasis in original).

With his prominence in the late 1960s and 1970s (and for excellent discussions of the goals and importance of Alinsky-style organizing, see Fisher, 1994, pp. 138–155; and Stein, 1986), the work of Alinsky and the IAF played a central role in the emergence of national groups such as the Association of Community Organizations for Reform Now (ACORN) and statewide groups such as Massachusetts Fair Share (Delgado, 1986; Perlman, 1979).

These groups were run by largely white, primarily middle-class staffs and organizers, and the organizers often had little experience with politics and conflict, except what they learned in their training by these groups. The model of organizing was basically the same in every locality: Local people would meet with organizers from the national organization to discuss their concerns and then work to mobilize larger numbers of people in those localities to address these problems. The national organizer, therefore, brings no agenda to the locality but instead allows the issues, and the solutions, to be defined by those within the locality. The recipe, therefore, was for a situation in which the IAF was working nationally to mobilize people, but its local-scale organizations, lacking any coherent ideological framework, became about neighborhoods "getting what they could." This, however, left them poorly positioned to deal with larger social forces, processes, and changes. In this model, the goals of community control and community empowerment remained, but rather than being seen as means to an end, they became ends in and of themselves. And in this way, it theoretically and practically overlapped with the neighborhood control movement of the late 1960s.

This left neighborhood organizations in the position of being particularly vulnerable to co-optation. This is essentially what happened as the 1980s emerged, and these groups evolved from confrontational organizations to developers. This evolution, which will be discussed shortly, was actually prefigured by the transformation of one of Alinsky's own groups in Chicago, The Woodlawn Organization (TWO). This organization, founded in 1961, was rather militant and held rent strikes and mobilized protests and picket lines, but by the early 1970s the organization had already been transformed into functionally acting as a CDC (Fish, 1973; Fisher, 1994; Jones, 1979). While the group realized early successes, it lacked enough vision to build on those successes when the area continued to decline and suffer from disinvestment and arson. Fish (1973) argued that the group's survival was an important achievement, but it is not clear how its survival affected any significant changes or even necessarily benefited the Woodlawn area.

To say, however, that politically progressive organizing did not occur in the 1970s would be both unfair and an oversimplification of local politics at the time. First, while the neo-Alinsky style organizers were self-avowedly "nonideological" in perspective, their goals of increased participation in, and the democratization of, urban politics were certainly laudable. They were also explicitly confrontational. They recognized that there are inherent conflicts in society, and understood that power is only appropriated through struggle. Second, there were powerful, community-based efforts to prevent the displacement of low-income residents by the continued construction of roads through inner-city neighborhoods, and by the last remnants of the Urban Renewal program's demolition (which formally ended in 1973 but, given the lag time associated with government construction projects, dragged on through to the late 1970s). Third, substantial political and legal victories were realized by those who struggled against the practice of financial institution redlining, and the efforts of these organizers yielded the 1975 passage of the Federal Home Mortgage Loan Disclosure Act and the 1977 Community Reinvestment Act (Squires, 1992).

CDCs: Professionalization and a New Generation

While the neighborhood movement was emerging in the 1970s, the older CDCs were themselves undergoing significant changes, with a new set of "2nd generation" (Peirce and Steinbach, 1987; Zdenek, 1987) CDCs growing from the roots of the antiredlining and urban renewal fights that had taken place. The older CDCs were facing uneven outcomes, as some grew while others failed. They shared a common experience, however, in which the sense of community control of enterprise continued to decline in importance as profit-making increasingly became the dominant goal. This was partly driven by the difficult realities of the markets these groups were operating within. This problem surfaced almost immediately (see Sturdivant, 1971), and continues today, but was also a function of the changing priorities of the OEO which, despite being on its last political legs, was still the dominant source of financial support for these "1st generation" CDCs. In one of the last policy statements from the OEO about the SIP program, issued in 1974, the agency stated, "All things being equal, ventures with a greater employment potential should be given higher priority than those with smaller employment potential, but in the short term job creation should not be pursued as an objective at the sacrifice of venture profits . . ." and "In order to produce benefits for low-income impact area residents, however, the institution-building and venture development efforts of the CDC require the participation of the non-poor in managerial and leadership roles" (quoted in Berndt, 1977, p. 137). The OEO, however, was not long for this world, and the Nixon administration terminated the agency and the CDC program was shifted to the newly created Community Services Administration. The first-generation CDCs were therefore left to deal with this loss of funding and, in accordance with the ideologies of black capitalism and the priorities that had been established by the OEO and President Nixon, they did so by becoming increasingly individualist and entrepreneurial in their orientation and goals.

Evaluations written during the 1970s, which for all intents and purposes were the first real evaluations of the CDCs created in the late 1960s, indicate the extent to which community control had become less important relative to the goal of economic development. Kelly (1977) conducted a survey of the members of the boards of directors of the CDCs created by OEO funding, and found that only 35 percent of the board members considered, "Providing opportunities for community-controlled ownership of businesses and property" one of their three highest priorities (Kelly, 1977, p. 25). In fact, in her analysis of community economic development, she plainly stated: "the community economic development movement in no way opposes or contradicts the American tradition of individual entrepreneurship" (Kelly, 1977, p. 21). A similar observation was made by Berndt (1977) who described the Bedford-Stuyvesant Restoration Corporation (the CDC that emerged from Robert Kennedy's tour through the neighborhood) as being run like General Motors. This should not have been surprising, because the people running it were the chair of Mobil Oil and the president of Citibank (Stoecker, 1997).

The second generation CDCs created in the late 1970s and the early 1980s came out of a different tradition from that of the first generation. Whereas the first generation was founded largely through government sponsorship, this second generation emerged out of protest movements that became organizations (see Piven and Cloward, 1977, for a useful framework for understanding the distinctions between movements and organizations). In becoming CDCs, they transformed themselves from being confrontational in their dealings with city governments, schools, banks and other local expressions of power, to cooperative in those relationships as they became more immersed in the structures against which they were originally protesting (Clarkson, 1987; Fulton, 1987; Gittell, 1980; Lenz, 1988).

Shelterforce magazine, one of the primary forums for discussion of CDCs and community organizing efforts, observed that there tended to be a three-step process to the transformation of oppositional community organizations to CDCs in the late 1970s and early 1980s. First, the groups emerge out of opposition to something (redlining, displacement, etc.). Second, the groups become somewhat more proactive, and begin direct political lobbying of city halls to enact their agendas. Third, the groups realize the limits of public money, and begin working to fulfill their agenda themselves (Fulton, 1987). While this description is a rather crude one, it nonetheless fairly accurately describes a process which was not actually one of political co-optation, but instead one of professionalization. These groups were not created to fundamentally transform the structures that govern the urbanization process. They emerged out of localized problems and conflicts, and it was not ideologically inconsistent to deal with local-scale problems as a developer rather than an adversarial activist. These transformations were not, therefore, normative. Instead they were merely programmatic.

Nonprofits for Hire: The 1980s and 1990s[1]

The 1980s and 1990s marked the coming of age for community development, as the number of CDCs grew rapidly, along with a heightened public awareness of their existence and activities and an increased set of burdens and expectations placed upon them. This growth of activity has been evident both in the number of CDCs and in their average size. While only about 150 first-generation CDCs were created in the late 1960s and early 1970s (and many failed within a few years), by the early 1980s another 500 to 750 second-generation CDCs had been created (Zdenek, 1987). The number of CDCs exploded in the 1980s, and an additional 1,000 CDCs were created between 1981 and 1987 (Peirce and Steinbach, 1987). The number of CDCs nationwide, therefore, essentially grew at modest, but significant, rate through the end of the 1960s and the 1970s, and beginning in the late 1970s and early 1980s began to grow much more rapidly. This growth continued through the decade, and by the early 1990s more than 2,000 were operating nationwide (de Souza Briggs and Mueller, 1997). This rapid growth has since continued, and there are currently roughly 3,600 CDCs (National Congress for Community Economic Development, 2002).

The growth of CDCs has been accompanied by significant changes in their structures, goals, and relationships with the public and private for-profit sectors. First, CDCs grew in the 1980s in spite of, and partially in reaction to, the shrinking desire of the public sector to provide goods of collective consumption—particularly affordable housing. The disappearance of Urban Development Action Grants (UDAGs) and project-based Section 8 funding are two of the most notable and visible examples of this decline in federal support for inner-city areas. Shrinking public resources left CDCs directly facing the impacts of these cutbacks, and thus helped create many more CDCs out of community-based political organizations. Local governments, as was discussed in chapter 1, exacerbated this loss of federal money by increasingly withdrawing from the provision of social services and housing in the 1980s. CDCs thus filled the vacuum left by the state—both at the local and federal levels. And while CDCs are rightfully best known for producing housing, their role is, and was, not limited to just affordable housing, as CDCs branched out into the areas of social-service provision, education, and health and child care (Vidal, 1996).

The second transformation emerges from the first. Because of the decline in public-sector support, funding for CDCs and CDC activities went from a "one-stop shopping" toward more "creative" forms of financing, often referred to as "patchwork" financing (Vidal, 1997). CDCs increasingly found themselves in the 1980s and 1990s putting together the funding for projects from a variety of sources, such as private investments made to receive a Low-Income Housing Tax Credit (after 1986), financial institution loans made to satisfy CRA requirements, grants from foundations, etc. This patchwork financing has furthered the process of professionalization in community development, because the financial-management capacities it requires greatly exceed those of the prior, single-source financing.

Such expertise has often come from the national intermediaries that were constructed in the late 1970s and early 1980s. In the space of four years, 1978–1981, the four most important intermediaries/foundations in community development were created. These are: the Neighborhood Reinvestment Corporation (NRC), formed by the federal government; the Local Initiatives Support Corporation (LISC), started by the Ford Foundation; the Fannie Mae Foundation, created by Fannie Mae; and the Enterprise Foundation, the product of real-estate magnate, and sometime urban utopian, Jim Rouse. Together they finance, provide technical assistance for, and generally shape the structure of the community-development industry. They are key institutions in both the growth of CDCs and in their increasing professionalization.

Together, this growing network of localized CDCs, their larger-scale foundation support, and other not-for-profit voluntary associations, have created a situation in which CDCs in many poor neighborhoods and localities have functionally become "the Shadow State" (Wolch, 1990). They provide the goods of collective consumption that formerly virtually defined municipal government functions. This role has been embraced not only by CDCs themselves, but by the state, as it willingly walks away from the provision of these services, and looks to the community-based sector to fill in the holes it has left behind (DeFilippis, 1997). It is also important to note that this public sector retreat, and the growth of the not-for-profit sector in public life, has been actively promoted by both the Democratic and Republican parties. And in 1996, while Newt Gingrich was wondering aloud about the movie *Boys Town* and the use of not-for-profit orphanages as a solution to the "problems" of children of welfare parents, president Clinton was leading a weekend-long celebration of "volunteerism" in Philadelphia. These events are merely emblematic, and represent the broad (if often only rhetorical) support for not-for-profits by both parties.

At the same time, most of whatever remained of the radical politics that were part of the context from which CDCs emerged in the 1960s, was lost, as they became increasingly part of the urban political machinery and political organizing receded further from their goals and mission. The Ford Foundation's definitive guide to community development in the 1980s put it—without any sense of apology: "with rare exceptions, the 1960s are now as much history for them (CDCs) as for the rest of American society. One can't very well hurl his body into the path of an oncoming bulldozer when he (or she) is the developer" (Peirce and Steinbach, 1987, p 8). That guide was tellingly called *Corrective Capitalism*.

Community Development Today

As has already been suggested, the community-development industry in the 1990s and 2000s has progressed along much the same lines that had been established in the earlier periods. In the last decade, the field has been dominated by various programmatic initiatives or trends focused on how to best go about "doing" community development. This has included discussions of "community-based assets," "capacity-building," "consensus organizing" and "social capital construction," among others. Rather than discuss these initiatives individually, it is perhaps more useful to explain the perspectives, aims, and objectives that they all share.

First, these initiatives are unambiguously market-based in their larger goals and programmatic details. This perspective has probably been made most explicit by Michael Porter through his Initiative for a Competitive Inner City and in a set of articles (Porter, 1995, 1997) which argued that, "a sustainable economic base can be created in inner cities only as it has been elsewhere: through private, for-profit initiatives, and investments based on economic self-interest and genuine competitive advantage" (Porter, 1997, p. 12). But Porter is far from alone in making these arguments, and the dominant argument at this point is that for CDCs to be successful, not only must they adopt an explicitly entrepreneurial set of goals and practices, but they must also work with the corporate sector (Bendick and Egan, 1991; Berger and Steinbach, 1992; Carr, 1999; Grogan and Proscio, 2000; Peirce and Steinbach, 1987; Taub, 1990; Tholin, 1994; Vidal, 1992, 1996). This point is highlighted by the trajectory of Paul Grogan, who was the president of LISC for over a decade and then founded CEOs for Cities (Herbert, 2001).

The second shared attribute of community development theory and practice in the last decade is a promotion of nonconfrontational forms of engagement and organizing. Community development is now a collaborative process, and the older, more conflictual ideals of black power, and neo-Alinsky-style organizing have been rejected (Epstein, 1996). Michael Eichler, the president of the Consensus Organizing Institute, which has received a great deal of attention in the field (see Gittell and Vidal, 1998), described a project that the Institute had worked on as having, "demonstrated the essential attribute of consensus organizing: instead of taking power from those who have it, consensus organizers build relationships in which power is shared for mutual benefit . . . Cooperation, rather than confrontation became the modus operandi for solving a neighborhood problem" (Eichler, 1998). Within the current understanding of cooperation, there is almost contempt for past organizing efforts, and Grogan and Proscio state, "The community organizing and planning of that period (the 1960s) was soon squandered on divisive or extremist political tactics, including the in-your-face style of protest that Tom Wolfe famously dubbed, 'mau-mauing' " (Grogan and Proscio, 2000, p. 66). The dominant understanding is thus that low-income inner-city residents have a shared set of interests with the larger society they exist within, and organizing and development should be structured accordingly. Power relations are therefore downplayed or completely ignored in this framework.

While it might seem a bit paradoxical, given the neo-liberal market orientation described above, the current period in community development is also characterized by a powerful reassertion of the idea of *community*, and a particular version of *communitarianism* (see Sites, 1998). This communitarian framework is one which posits a belief that there are shared interests among individuals in a community, and thus community development should be about creating the social relationships that allow those mutual goals to be realized. This form of communitarianism thus mirrors consensus-based organizing, in that the assumption is of shared interests; the difference is one assumes it for relations between people in the community and the rest of the world, and the other for relations between people within a community. There are two principal figures in this understanding of community. The first is John McKnight, who has argued for a framework of community development centered around "community-based assets" (Kretzman and McKnight, 1993; McKnight, 1995; see also Shragge and Fisher, 2001). The second is Robert Putnam, whose work on social capital (Putnam, 1995, 1996, 2000) has become almost axiomatic in community-development theory and practice (see DeFilippis, 2001). Not only do both of them argue that relations within communities tend to be largely "win-win" relations, but both take that framework one step farther to assume that *individual* gains and interests in the community are synonymous with *collective*, or community, gains and interests. Both also largely assume that communities are functions of, and defined by, the attributes and relationships of people within them. Thus not only does this particular form of communitarianism fit with consensus or nonconfrontational organizing, but it also fits with the neoliberal, market-based perspectives and policies that govern community development activity.

Together these three perspectives, which dominate the theory and practice of community development, can best be described as a form of *neoliberal communitarianism*. This neoliberal communitarianism has, at its core, a belief that society is conflict-free, and it gets this from both halves of its theoretical framework. It also represents the fruition of the depoliticization of community development that came with its split from community organizing in the late 1960s. This depoliticization also needs to be understood as both a product, and producer, of their support from the public sector. The political logic of CDCs in American politics has therefore come full circle. The federal government, which initiated the movement for community development by sponsoring often radical political organizations working toward community control and empowerment, now supports CDCs exactly because they are no longer connected to any radical political movement. And the goals of CDCs have also come full circle. Initially conceived as vehicles that would use the market as a means to the end of community empowerment and control, they have now become vehicles for the market, in which the goal of community control is not even an issue.

Problems in Neoliberal Communitarian Community Development Theory and Practice

All of this would be fine, and not warrant any objection here, if this understanding of community development had demonstrated itself capable of accomplishing the two goals of this project: to allow low-income people to have more control over their economic lives, and to do so in ways which equitably improve the lives of people in low-income communities. Unfortunately, it has failed in achieving, or moving toward, both of these goals. Admittedly, community development has produced a substantial volume of adequate affordable housing for low-income people over the last thirty years. And certainly the lives of thousands of low-income people have benefited significantly because of this. But all too often, the reality has been that community-development efforts have failed to visibly or measurably improve the larger communities in which they are located. Instead, we are faced, as Lenz put it, with "the terrible paradox of thriving organizations and dying communities," or, more morbidly, "the operation was successful, but the patient died" (Lenz, 1988, p. 25). The persistence of these problems led Stoecker to observe that "the continuing critiques of CDCs across three decades suggest that more is at issue than imperfect practice" (Stoecker, 1997, p. 4). He is certainly right. The problems are much more fundamental and require a complete rethinking of community development. Community development needs to reconnect with its goals of community control, but it must do in a way that understands capital, capitalism, and class in American society.

The theoretical problems relate to both halves of the neoliberal communitarian framework, and they will be addressed in turn. First, the interests of capital should not be assumed to be synonymous with the interests of communities. I do not subscribe to the view that capital and community *necessarily* have the diametrically opposing interests of exchange value and use value (respectively), and some forms of capital are very much *within* communities. But given the lack of capital owned and controlled by low-income people, however, the use value vs. exchange value is usually the case. Capital is interested in the extraction of profit, which is needed to reproduce itself and to generate wealth for the *individuals* who own it. This is inherently true in capitalism. We should no more assume the shared interests of black inner-city business owners and their workers than we would the shared interests of Nike and its sweatshop workers in Indonesia. And while both the local business owners and their workers might share an interest in a community (because of their local dependence on it), that in no way eliminates their inherent respective class interests.

Second, capitalism is about competition—both between and within classes. And while capitalist economies are not zero-sum games, they still, like all forms of competition, unquestionably produce winners and losers. Given this reality, it is exceedingly unlikely that low-income people in inner-city areas would be able to succeed in many competitions with their wealthier, better-educated, and more politically powerful, suburban (or urban gentrifier) counterparts. This is especially true if the playing field for the competition is the free market, which has already produced such uneven results. Uneven development is an inherent component of capitalism, and one of the primary geographic manifestations of its competitive structure. Only by ignoring this geographical and historical truism can we assume that underdeveloped places and spaces can be developed by the free market for the gains of people within them.

Third, given the histories of capital disinvestment and decline in most inner-city neighborhoods, more often than not, any investment capital in them will need to come from the outside. The potential for inner-city residents to control their own economic lives therefore immediately gets undercut by a framework that relies on free-market investments into the inner-city. Embracing the market leaves control over capital and economic development firmly and squarely beyond the reach of people in the inner-city.

The communitarian half of the framework is comparably fundamentally flawed, and in similar ways. First, the individual is *not* the same as the group. We cannot assume that individual gains and interests are the same as those of the larger community. This point is especially valid in low-income urban neighborhoods. As Blakely and Small astutely observe in their critique of Porter, "there is little connection between [individual] work and better outcomes for ghetto dwellers or for their communities. The signals are very clear. To move up economically requires moving out. As a result, the link between job and social betterment is lost collectively as achievers move out of the ghetto" (Blakely and Small, 1995/1996, p. 166).

Second, the communitarian perspective assumes that people in a community share common interests simply by virtue of living in the same area. But clearly communities are diverse, conflict-laden, and contested places and spaces. For interests to be shared requires the construction of shared interests—not the a priori assumption of their existence. Landlords and renters, business owners and workers, and service providers and recipients are all fairly obvious examples of how interests are not shared by people in a community. They demonstrate that individuals' self-interest cannot be "added up" to yield a community's interests. Not only does this assumption of shared or mutual interests deny the various forms of exploitation and conflict that occur between people in a community, it also ignores how oppressive communities can be to people who are in some way defined as "different" (see Young, 1990, for a thorough discussion of these issues).

Third, communities are not simply the products of the attributes of the people within them. Instead, as was discussed in chapter 1, for localities, communities are the products of a complex set of much larger-scale social relationships. Citibank (for instance) and its lending practices, state governments and their education financing policies, communities with soon-to-be emigrants in other countries, are all very real examples of how America's urban communities are products of a whole host of relations that extend geographically well beyond the place of the community. These relations are often contentious (school funding issues being a classic example), and are always imbued with issues of power. Only by ignoring these vitally important, power-laden connections can we assume that communities are the products of the attributes of the individuals that live and work within them.

Along with concerns over the processes of globalization and capital mobility, it was in reaction to this fundamentally flawed framework for community development that this current project emerged. But this is also why the failures of the 1960s community control efforts warranted such attention here. At the substantial risk of telescoping history, the current problems of CDCs stem from the flaws of the framework that inspired their formation. The contemporary forms of community development only represent a deepening of those problems—not their creation.

Concluding Comments

I want to end this chapter by discussing three moments from 1999, which highlight the contemporary political state of community development. The first is an extended memo in the *Neighborworks Journal*, which is the journal of the NRC, by James Carr, senior vice-president of the Fannie Mae Foundation. In it he issued a call for "A New Paradigm for Community Reinvestment." The new paradigm called for greater collaboration between community developers and outside investors and businesses. It included a promotion of the idea of place-marketing in which community development projects could take on names such "The Woodlands," "Celebration" and "Redwood Shores." He even stated, "some of these places could be treated as urban blank slates, where the development takes on an image the investors choose" (Carr, 1999, p. 21). In this new paradigm, the first role for government is to, "assist private firms to extract value from community assets" (Carr, 1999, p. 22)—which is a far cry from government supporting community control or equitable development.

The second "moment" comes from the substantial gutting of the Community Reinvestment Act, which occurred in the fall of 1999. The CRA was a product of long-standing community organizing efforts in the 1970s, and its enactment as a national regulatory policy in 1977 needs to be understood as a major victory for organizers at the time. After years of political pressure from banks to eliminate it, or substantially mitigate its regulatory powers, the fight came to a head in 1999. The problem was that by 1999 the community organizations that had worked so hard to see it enacted had long since become CDCs. As such, they were unable or unwilling to mobilize much constituency to save it. To be fair, ACORN did have some demonstrations and protests, but the political battle was largely waged as one of "our lobbyists" vs. "their lobbyists." The outcome, therefore, was never seriously in doubt.

Finally, that summer I was at a meeting at the Urban Justice Center in New York planning a march from Washington, D.C., to New York City as part of the now-international Economic Human Rights Campaign. In the course of the discussion, one of the issues that arose was contacting other community organizations who might be sympathetic to the march in order to solicit their support. One of the people in the room (John Krinsky, who had researched Mutual Housing Associations and Community Land Trusts, while at the Community Service Society—see chapter 4) suggested that one of the groups we should contact about this march was the Association of Neighborhood and Housing Development (ANHD). ANHD is the principal trade association for CDCs in New York City. The response from the roomful of thirty local community and political organizers to the mention of its name was a unanimous, "Who?"

CHAPTER 3

Collective Ownership of Work

*Could there be a better answer to the stupidity of Karl Marx, than millions
of workers individually sharing in the ownership of the means of production?*
—Ronald Reagan[1]

*However excellent in principle, and useful in practice, [cooperative factories]
will never be able to arrest the growth in geometrical progression of monopoly,
to free the masses, nor even to perceptibly lighten the burden of their miseries.*
—Karl Marx[2]

While the bulk of this book will deal with efforts for local control that have
emerged from the community development movement, there is a parallel
set of efforts for local control that instead has come from places of employment. These efforts share a lot with the community-based efforts that will
be discussed in chapters 4 and 5, but rely on forms of worker ownership to
allow people to realize local control over their economic lives. There is, of
course, a long history to worker ownership in the United States, but the
role and political meaning of worker-ownership have been significantly
transformed in this era of economic globalization.

This chapter will begin by briefly discussing the particular implications
economic globalization has had for American workers. This is followed by
a discussion of the history of worker ownership—with a particular emphasis on its politics. It then describes the structure and economic performance of the two most common forms of worker ownership: worker
cooperatives and Employee Stock Ownership Plans (ESOPs). It then uses a
few case studies to illuminate the issues involved in worker ownership. The
first is a brief case of Cooperative Home Care Associates, a worker-cooperative of home health-care workers in the Bronx, New York, and the second

is the much longer case study of a worker-buyout of a factory in Pittsfield, Massachusetts. Together these highlight the potential, limits, and contradictions of worker ownership in the United States.

Economic Restructuring and the State of American Workers

There are several ways that the impacts of economic restructuring and globalization have been felt by American workers. Rather than discuss these thoroughly and completely (which has been very capably done by Moody, 1997, among others), I'm going to simply pull out a few of the key ways in which American workers have been effected by economic change.

The most publicly visible of the impacts of the economic restructuring of the past twenty-five years has probably been the substantial decline of many older industrial regions, localities, and worksites. The American public sphere was inundated with images of plant closures and communities decimated through the 1970s, 1980s, and the first half of the 1990s. This was, in short, the creation of "the rustbelt" in the United States. But the changes in the American economy extended beyond simply regional decline in the industrial Midwest, to a broader process of the loss of industrial employment in the American economy. Manufacturing employment fell from 28 percent of total U.S. employment in 1965 to 22 percent in 1980, and less than 15 percent in 2000 (Rowthorn and Ramaswamy, 1997; and Statistical Abstract of the United States, 2001). There were several causes of this deindustrialization, but the primary issues were increased transportation and communication capabilities, coupled with a deskilling of some labor processes, had allowed for capital to be disinvested from productive capacity in older industrial plants. Industrial capital is thereafter redirected to either investment in the global periphery, like Thailand, or to what had traditionally been peripheral areas within the core economies, like rural North Carolina (see Massey, 1984, for an excellent analysis of these processes). There was, in short, a disassociation of industrial capital from the places that had fostered the accumulation and reproduction of that capital throughout the "Fordist" period of the twentieth century.[3] This spatial separation between industrial places and industrial capital is therefore both a cause of this disinvestment (Meek, Woodworth, and Dyer, 1988; Megson and O'Toole, 1993) and, at the same time, an outcome of that disinvestment (Raines, Berson and Gracie, 1982), as the older factories were further disinvested in, the more removed from the control of industrial capital they became. In most popular and academic understandings of these issues, workers and communities are virtually powerless in the face of this footloose industrial capital, and are rather helpless as it closes factories, eliminates jobs, and devastates the lives of people and the regions.

Along with these processes of deindustrialization has come the growth of the service sector, and service-sector employment[4] grew from 29 million people, or less than 29 percent of total employment, in 1980 to almost 50 million people (37 percent) in 2000 (Statistical Abstract of the United States, 2001). Service sector employment tends to be both lower paying, and less unionized, and so it has left American workers more vulnerable, and meant that the pretax and posttax incomes of many working Americans have fallen dramatically over the last twenty-five years (see Hartman, 2001; Shapiro, Greenstein, and Primus, 2001, for good data on this).

Finally, the period of globalization and capital mobility has brought with it the increased prominence of the goal of "flexibility" and workers are increasingly required to function accordingly—this is true for the skills workers are expected to possess, the tasks they are expected to perform, and, most importantly, the hours they are expected to work. While labor has always been a commodity in capitalism, it is increasingly being treated solely as such—separate from all of the other qualities that are inherent in labor, and that come from the fact that labor is human beings and not just an input into production. This is most apparent in the growth of temporary work in American labor, and almost 30 percent of all workers in the United States work in jobs that are not permanent, full-time jobs (National Alliance for Fair Employment, 2002). Temporary workers, like migrant farmworkers, are almost the purest form of labor as a commodity and input into production, because—in the name of flexibility—owners get the labor power they need, when they need it, can rid themselves of the costs of labor power when they don't need it, and certainly do not need to pay for all of the long-term social costs involved in the reproduction of that labor power (particularly health-care costs, which are a significant component of most businesses' labor costs).

The extent to which all of these changes can be attributed to the increased globalization of economic activity and growth in capital mobility is unclear. And it has been argued that deindustrialization and changes in the labor market are only slightly *directly* attributed to globalization and its attendant processes (see Krugman, 1996; and Walker, 1999, for two very different perspectives that happen to share this argument). But the empirical validity of the role of globalization in the devaluation, and growing insecurity of American labor is not the point here. Rather, it is the potential for mobility—or, more often, the threat of mobility—and the all-encompassing language and excuse of "global competition" that have too often been enough to disempower working-class people and communities. This has left local workers unable to bargain with their larger-scale corporate bosses, and with standards of living and a quality of life often much worse than they had enjoyed in the past.

The solutions to the increasing disempowerment of local workers and communities has often come in the form of workers coming together to collectively own their place of work. Or, similarly, local people coming together to create a collectively owned business, in order to keep control, and profits, in the hands of the workers and within the community. This, of course, is not a new solution or ownership structure, and there is a long history of collective ownership of workplaces in the American economy. It is to this history that we now turn.

The History, Structures, and Politics of Worker-Ownership

As the organization of production in the United States was transformed away from home-based to industry-based in the mid- to late-nineteenth-century, worker ownership emerged as an important component of labor's strategy to realize greater control in the face of these changes. This was primarily in the craft unions, but also in the larger industrial unions as well. At least 135 cooperatives were established by the Knights of Labor (the predecessor of the American Federation of Labor), between 1878 and 1886 (Logue and Yates, 1999). While most of the cooperatives failed, the idea of worker-cooperatives resurfaced sporadically through the first third of the twentieth century. This was particularly true during periods of recession and high unemployment. The most significant example was the creation of cooperatives in the plywood industry in the Pacific Northwest during the Great Depression. This cluster of cooperatives, the largest in the United States, thrived until as recently as the recession of the early 1990s when many of them finally succumbed to changes in the global market and emerging environmental regulations that limited the accessibility of timber in the Northwest (Gunn, 1992).

Despite the cooperatives established during the 1930s, worker-ownership generally faded after the Great Depression, as labor and capital largely agreed to a collective bargaining framework that was, for a time, able to benefit the workers who had access to union membership (which was, of course, only a particular segment of the working class). After 1974, when Congress passed legislation that provided tax breaks for employee ownership, worker-ownership reemerged as both a strategy for labor and as a component of the American economic landscape. It did so, however, not in the form of the older worker cooperatives but instead as Employee Stock Ownership Plans (ESOPs).

ESOPs

The primary form that worker-ownership currently takes is that of the ESOP. ESOPs represent a fairly significant portion of the American economy. The most recent estimates indicate that there are about 11,000 ESOPs in the United States, with about 7.7 million employees participating in these plans. Of the 11,000, it is estimated that only 2,500, or 23 percent, are majority employee-owned (Logue and Yates, 1999, p. 227), so most ESOPs do not represent employee ownership or control. And the evidence very strongly suggests that minority employee-owned firms are not much more participatory than traditionally owned firms (see "New Study Shows Public Employee Ownership Firms Not More Participative," 1997). Instead ESOPs function as benefits packages, and they are often created to prevent a hostile takeover by placing stock in "friendly" hands.

Technically, an ESOP is an employee benefit package that is governed by the 1974 Employee Retirement Income Security Act (ERISA). ESOPs, however, are very different from most of the benefit packages (like pension funds) governed by this act. An ESOP is a trust fund that is separate from both the employees and the company, and unlike most trust funds can borrow money from banks and other investors in order to acquire (or create) a company. When this occurs, the ESOP is referred to as a "leveraged ESOP," and this is the form taken by most majority- or wholly worker-owned firms.[5] The ESOP then acquires the shares of the firm and distributes them to employees based on seniority or salary. The emphasis on seniority means that the longer workers are with the firm, the greater the number of shares they receive annually. When workers retire or otherwise leave the firm, they can either sell their shares on the market (if the corporation is public) or, since most ESOPs are closely held and small in scale, sell the shares back to the firm at their "Fair Market Value" (which is determined annually by an independent auditor).

Worker compensation in an ESOP is somewhat different than it is in other, traditionally owned firms. In most firms, employees earn a salary and benefits (such as payments to a pension fund *if* they receive benefits). In ESOPs the workers receive their salaries, the long-term capital of the stocks, *and* a share in the company's profits, if there are any. So workers in ESOPs have both long-term and short-term interests in their companies' success.

When it comes to the performance of ESOPs relative to their traditionally owned competitors, the evidence is clear: ESOPs perform better than their competitors (Conte and Svejnar, 1990; Hollod, 1999; Logue and Yates, 1999; Rosen, Klein and Young, 1986). More importantly, participatory ESOPs perform better than nonparticipatory ESOPs (Logue and Yates, 1999; Rosen, Klein and Young, 1986; U.S. GAO, 1987; Winther and Marens, 1997). There is much debate about why this is. Theories range from the increased morale that can accompany ownership, to employees making rational decisions about working harder to improve their stock values, to workers constructing a set of peer pressures to insure that coworkers are doing their jobs as well. For purposes of this study, the exact causes of the increased productivity and profitability of employee-owned companies is not the issue, but rather that profitability is in-and-of-itself a verification of the viability of this model and its uses in capitalist economies.

Worker Cooperatives

Worker cooperatives are perhaps the purest forms of economic democracy currently operating in the United States. Unilike ESOPs, worker cooperatives have democratic structures of governance built into their model of corporate ownership. There are two core characteristics that tend to be shared by all worker cooperatives. The first is the principle of "one person, one vote." That is, once a worker becomes a member of the cooperative, they possess voting rights as an equal with every other member. The second is that any profits of the cooperative are shared among the worker-member-owners on the basis of the workers' pay, or hours worked, or both. Only persons who work in a cooperative can be a member of it, and therefore the principal is one of labor employing capital, rather than capital employing labor (see Adams and Hanson, 1992, chapter 2).

One of the keys to the operation of worker cooperatives is the system of internal capital accounts, which was developed in the Mondragon cooperatives in the Basque country in Spain. This system allows for members to move on or retire, and provides for the self-interest of the current workers to be coincident with that of future workers. Despite the democratic character of worker-cooperatives, their potential in the face of capital mobility and globalization, the utility of the internal capital accounts structure, and the growth of supportive intermediaries dedicated to promoting and providing assistance to worker-cooperatives, the number of these types of businesses has not grown dramatically over the last twenty years. In fact, the total number of cooperatives in the country, around 200, is probably less than it was in the 1970s (Krimerman, 1999). Perhaps this is because while ESOPs have enjoyed a great deal of political support, which has yielded favorable public-policy decisions about how they are taxed, cooperatives have not had such political backing, and have largely been outside of the radar of contemporary American politics and economics.

The Politics of Worker-Ownership

The politics of worker-ownership defy easy description, and require some discussion here. As this chapter's introductory quotes would suggest, the promotion of worker-ownership has come more visibly from the right than from the left in the United States (Adams and Ellerman, 1989; Gamble and Kelly, 1996; Prude, 1984). The primary intellectual and political driving force behind the expansion of worker ownership in the late nineteenth century came from two sources: 1) liberals who recognized that capitalism would lead to a concentration of property wealth so unequal that it would threaten the legitimacy of capitalism itself; and 2) "populist" liberals (in the tradition of Jefferson) who argued that the concentration of property wealth was unjust in and of itself, primarily because it prevented people from participating in the process of democracy (Russell, 1984). The arguments of both these schools applied not only to real property but also to nonagricultural productive, or industrial, property.

In the twentieth century, the idea of worker-ownership reemerged largely because of the work of two men who personify these two nineteenth-century positions: Louis Kelso and Russell Long. Louis Kelso was an investment banker and believer in capitalism, but he was not blind to its contradictions. In his definitive work, *The Capitalist Manifesto* (Kelso and Adler, 1958), he made the argument that in order for capitalism to survive, it needed more capitalists, and that the logical place for these capitalists to come from was the ranks of labor. In this way, the tendency within capitalism to move toward monopoly could be offset. Also, worker-ownership would have the further benefit to capital of making labor more docile—in ways not dissimilar from homeownership's political effects. Russell Long was a senator from Louisiana, and the son of the populist governor Huey Long. His father's son, Russell Long believed in the goal of a wide distribution of ownership and control. His efforts led to the legislation in 1974 that created the ESOP structure, with its associated tax benefits.

The left has been much more ambivalent about worker ownership, both historically and in the contemporary period (much of that ambivalence stems from exactly the qualities that neoliberals find so appealing). Despite early on having been impressed with the small-scale communes he and Engels found in the U.S. in the 1840s (see Feuer, 1966), by the time he spoke to the First International, Marx had come to view industrial cooperatives as a way to deal with the manifested contradictions and injustices of capital, without fundamentally transforming their cause. Along with the quote that introduces this chapter, Marx went on to state, "it is perhaps for this reason that plausible nobleman, philanthropic middle class spouters, and even keen political economists, have all at once turned nauseously complimentary to the very cooperative labor system they had vainly tried to nip in the bud" (Tucker, 1972, p. 380). Most Marxists accepted this analysis and support for worker-cooperatives on the left was therefore undercut very early in their history. Marx's condemning criticisms at the First International notwithstanding, there has been some support among leftists for small-scale worker-ownership.

The most forceful promotion of worker-ownership from the left has come from those who saw the central relation in capitalism as the buying and selling of labor power (and not the private—that is, not-public—ownership of the means of production). The solution to this exploitative relationship was found in a decentered socialism, in which workers owned and controlled the means of production via the individual factories in which they worked. Perhaps the most common expressions of this view of worker ownership in the West came from the Italian Syndicalists (like Labriola and Orano) and the British Guild Socialists (primarily Cole) (see Schecter, 1994, for useful summaries of both these movements). The model of Market Socialism in Yugoslavia during Tito's regime came out of a similar understanding of capitalism and socialism (see Pateman, 1970). And while the Yugoslav experiment was unsuccessful in many ways, the end of "state socialism" in the Soviet Union and Eastern Europe has opened a space for some leftists to reclaim the ideas of "market socialism" (see Miller, 1990; Roemer, 1994; Roosevelt and Belkin, 1994; Schweieckart, 1993; Yunker, 1992). But those movements were fairly peripheral to the left in the United States, and never received a lot of attention there. As Adams and Ellerman (1989, p. 14), of the Industrial Cooperatives Association, have argued "For much of the Left . . . worker ownership is 'private' (in the sense of being non-government) and therefore suspect. When 'workers' get together with 'ownership' the Left wants to send along 'the community' as a chaperone."

Worker Buyouts to Prevent Plant Closures

The politics of worker-ownership began to change in the 1970s and 1980s as a result of the economic restructuring of that period. A new generation of leftists have come to promote worker-ownership as an issue of geographic scale and local control (Adams and Ellerman, 1989; Benello, 1992; DiGiovanna, 1997; Gunn and Gunn, 1991; Lynd, 1987; Megson and O'Toole, 1993; Olson, 1986–87; Shuman, 1998; Wilkenson and Quarter, 1996)—and it is to these voices that I'm adding mine. These leftists have usually used the language of "anchoring capital in communities" (Olson, 1986–87) and the Industrial Cooperatives Association—one the strongest advocates for democratic worker-ownership—has called worker-ownership the "vehicle for community development and local economic control" (Megson and O'Toole, 1993). The most visible form in which worker-ownership has been utilized to address issues of geographic scale and empower local control has been the buying of plants that are threatened with closure by their "parent," usually multiplant, firms.

Perhaps the most famous instance of a worker buyout was the case of Weirton Steel in Weirton, West Virginia, in 1984, which garnered significant national attention (*Newsweek,* 1983; Prude, 1984; Varano, 1999; *Wall Street Journal,* 1983; Zukin, 1991, ch. 4). The case was actually rather unsuccessful and not only did the workers have to make significant long-term wage and benefit concessions, but they have also realized very little of the control promised to them. The outcome in Weirton, unfortunately, is not unique, and many buyouts that were organized to avoid a plant closure have not been successful in either establishing worker control or keeping the plant open (see Logue and Yates, 1999; Winther and Marens, 1997, for documentation of the performance of closure-avoiding buyouts). Accordingly, many unions have been skeptical about the use of employee buyouts. This is because if the buyout fails to keep the plant open, it has liberated the parent company from its financial responsibilities to the workers (in terms of unemployment payments and pension fund compensation), and the workers might actually lose a good deal of money by virtue of their buyout (see McElrath and Rowan, 1992 for a summary of American labor's conflicted views on employee buyouts). This is especially significant in cases where the workers use their own capital (either through their pension funds or personal savings or both) as an important component of the financing of the buyout.

In a large study of failed worker-owned firms (of which many had been bought by their employees to prevent plant closure) the Worker Ownership Institute found that, "By and large they fail for the same reason as conventionally run firms: poor management compounded with inability to master the market" (Logue, Glass, Patton, Teodosio and Thomas, 1998). One of the key questions, therefore, that needs to be addressed when assessing the desirability of a buyout is whether the plant threatened by closure is being closed because the market has changed and it is no longer profitable, and not likely to be profitable again. Or, conversely, if the plant is being closed because it is not profitable enough to fit into the larger-scale plans of a national or multinational multiplant corporation. The evidence on plant closures over the last twenty years has left little doubt that plant closures in multiplant firms often occur *despite the profitability of the plant being closed* (Bluestone, 1989; Harrison and Bluestone, 1988; Howland, 1987; Kirkham and Watts, 1997). Such closures are more about the using of space to discipline labor (Massey, 1984) than about issues of corporate profitability. So while worker-ownership of a plant is, from the perspective of the workers, theoretically more desirable than that plant's closure, the market context of the plant being threatened, and the conditions of worker-ownership, must be understood before any buyout effort is undertaken.

With this background, we will turn to a couple of cases of worker-ownership. The first being Cooperative Home Care Associates, a worker-cooperative in the South Bronx, and the other, in much greater depth, being the workers' buyout of Marland Mold in Pittsfield, Massachusetts.

Cooperative Home Care Associates

Cooperative Home Care Associates (CHCA) was founded in 1985 in the South Bronx in a local context of widespread poverty and unemployment (see chapter 5 for a more thorough description of the area at this time), and a national situation in which changes in Medicare policy were moving senior citizens out of hospital beds and into their private homes. As a result of the burgeoning population of people in need of home health-care workers, this sector grew dramatically through the 1980s, and that growth has continued to this day. From 1988 to 1998, the number of home health-care workers nationwide grew by 40 percent, and demand for them in the future is predicted to grow by 58 percent from 1998 to 2008 (Scanlon, 2001). In many ways home health-care workers are the "temp" workers of the health-care industry, and their growth reflects both the growth in subcontracting out of services so common in the contemporary economy and the shrinking of the state—through Medicare policies—which is the principal cause of their existence. Wages for workers in the industry therefore are limited, and the median wages for the industry of slightly under eight dollars an hour are about 30 percent less than the median wage for all workers in the country (American Federation of State, County and Municipal Employees, 2001). More important than the hourly wage is the fact that the working hours are largely irregular and, more often than not, home care workers work less than full-time. The workers are overwhelmingly female and disproportionately black (often recent immigrants from the Caribbean) or Latina. The work is also very individualized and the greatest interaction the workers have is not with their coworkers or supervisors (their agency nurses and coordinators), but with their clients in their homes. It has therefore been a notoriously difficult industry to unionize, and the benefits of union successes in the health-care industry often do not make it to these workers, since they largely contract with private agencies rather than directly with the public sector.

This then is the context in which CHCA was created: a neighborhood in free fall and in a growing industry whose growth was largely built on the exploitation of the workers involved. The founding of CHCA was not done without support, however, and the Community Service Society of New York (CSS), along with technical assistance from the ICA Group and some financial support from the Charles Stewart Mott Foundation, played an active role in its creation. Despite this assistance, CHCA struggled in its first few years—failing to either improve the wages and working conditions (hours and benefits) of its employees, or make a profit. This led to a major reorganization of the management and Rick Surpin, who had been at CSS providing technical assistance, became the CEO—a position he held until 2000 (although he still chairs the company's board). In the years following, CHCA grew, and by 1990 was majority worker-owned. It also began to introduce wage increases for more difficult jobs and weekend work, and improved its introductory and continuing training capacities—and thus brought something like a career ladder to a job that has traditionally not had one. Its growth led to increased interest and support from outside foundations—and its 1991-created not-for-profit affiliate worked to reproduce the model in other cities. In 1993 Home Care Associates of Philadelphia was created, and the following year Cooperative Home Care of Boston (CHCB) was founded. Together the three became the Cooperative Healthcare Network, which now has smaller training programs running in Detroit, Michigan, and Pine Bluff, Arkansas.

CHCA itself has continued to grow and expand, and currently employs 650 women, of which 70 percent are worker-owners (Cooperative Home Care Associates, 2002). Shares are worth $1,000 and have paid dividends that average between $200 and $400 per year. Share ownership requires a $50 down payment and weekly payments of $3.65 (but voting rights come with the $50 down payment). The majority of the board of directors comes from the ranks of the workers, and, like all worker-cooperatives, the board is voted on with the one-worker, one-vote structure. Daily management decisions, however, are the domain of the management—and while there is an elected Worker Council, there is also serious debate among the workers about whether or not to join the Service Employees International Union (SEIU). Wages average $8.20 an hour, which is only slightly better than the industry standard—and lack of union membership meant that the workers were not able to benefit from the deal reached between SEIU local 1199 and New York governor George Pataki in 2002. Management, typically, is not supportive of the decision to unionize, but does not appear to be fighting it, should the workers decide to do so. Importantly, CHCA guarantees its workers at least 30 hours per week and provides health insurance, and paid sick and vacation time—all relative rarities in the sector. Worker turnover therefore hovers at around 20 percent, which is less than half the industry average. In general, CHCA can be described as a strong and growing company that has weathered some early problems, as well as changes in the marketplace for its service, to be a model in its industry. Some of its affiliates, however, have not faired as well.

In December 1999, the CHCB closed after being in operation for almost six years—and being consistently profitable until late 1997. The reasons for this closure are several and include internal management problems—particularly a poorly handled leadership transition in early 1998—and external. Most important of the external sources were the cuts in Medicare funding that came from the Balanced Budget Act of 1997, and which cut Medicare funding for home care services by a total of 45 percent in the three subsequent years (Paraprofessional Healthcare Institute, 2000).[6] The ultimate responsibility for this lies with the government, and surely the government has to be willing to provide the resources necessary for senior citizens to receive the health-care services they need (and in this sense the overall exploitation of home health-care workers is, at root, a function of government policies). At the same time, however, CHCB could not diversify its market away from subcontracting for Medicare-receiving agencies rapidly enough, and by 1999 the company joined the ranks of closures that resulted from this policy shift. In short, the company closed because the market environment in which it was operating changed, and its management was unable to adapt and survive.

Marland Mold, Inc.

Pittsfield, Massachusetts[7]

Pittsfield, Massachusetts is a small city (which has had about 50,000 people since World War II) in the heart of Berkshire County in Western Massachusetts. The story of Pittsfield is a fairly typical one. Its nineteenth-century history is one of a transformation from an agricultural city to an industrial one, and its twentieth-century history is one of industrial growth, stability, and then decline. While its history is one of a predominantly blue-collar labor force, the city's workers are now predominantly employed in the service sectors. General Electric Plastics entered the town in 1903, and the economic history of the town has been closely linked to the company ever since. Pittsfield, via GE, became a center for the plastics industry (Nash, 1989). But beginning in the 1970s and 1980s, the company began to relocate production elsewhere, and the number of production workers declined. This was further exacerbated by the cutbacks in military contracts of the late 1980s and early 1990s. The town's recent history is therefore one of plant closures, industrial disinvestment, and deindustrialization.

The Company

Marland Mold, Inc., is a class-A, single-source mold maker specializing in high-cavitation molds. The company produces steel molds for the consumer food and beverage industry (plastic soda bottles and caps), the medical and pharmaceutical industry (plastic tubes, flasks, etc.), and for the household chemical and cleanser industry (detergent bottles and caps). Like most firms in this "bottom feeder" (Pryweller, 1999) component of the much larger plastics industrial sector, it is a relatively small company (Bradley, 1999), with a total workforce that has ranged in the last twenty-five years from thirty employees to about a hundred and fifty. The workforce of the plant is divided into three types of workers: management, salaried workers, and hourly workers. The hourly workers, who constitute the vast majority of the plant's workforce (roughly 75 percent) are skilled machinists who work with a capital-intensive set of molding machines. The hourlies must therefore successfully complete a two-year apprenticeship program in order to be qualified to work for the firm, and the company has created such a program with the local high schools in order to insure a consistent supply of new workers in the plant, which employs many of the same hourlies that it had twenty-five years ago. Like Pittsfield itself, the workforce is almost entirely white, and in my visits there I only saw one black employee, who was an hourly. It is also a very masculine space, as the only female employees are administrators and one manager. It is, in short, almost a caricature of the old, unionized, American industrial plant.

History

Marland Mold was founded in 1946 by two machinists who had worked at GE Plastics. The founders began the company in their garage, but it grew fairly rapidly, and they hired their first employee in 1948. The company continued to grow for the next twenty years, but when the founders retired in 1969, they sold it to Valve Corp. of America (Cuyler, 1991a). A few years later, Valve Corp. was bought by Ethyl Corp., and the plant became Ethyl Marland. The plant remained in Ethyl's hands until 1989, when it was spun off into the newly created Tredegar Molded Products in Richmond, Virginia, a wholly owned subsidiary of Ethyl Corp. which included Ethyl's twelve mold-making plants. In short, Marland followed a typical route from being a small independent local company, to just another branch plant in a large multinational.

These transactions left the local Pittsfield plant in a situation of dependence on the multinational Tredegar, for several reasons. First, the plant no longer handled marketing and possessed a limited sales department with only two employees, as these functions were centralized at the corporate headquarters in Richmond. Its ability to bid independently for work orders was therefore very limited. Second, and because of this, much of the plant's work originated at Tredegar, and therefore the plant essentially fared only as well, or as poorly, as its corporate owners. Third, Tredegar headquarters made decisions about which plants should receive work orders and which would not, and so not only was the Pittsfield plant limited in its ability to bid for orders, and therefore dependent on orders coming through corporate headquarters, but it also had little control over whether those work orders came to it or one of Tredager's eleven other plants.

These intrafirm relationships also rendered the location of the plant almost irrelevant—at least economically. Marland had originally relied on General Electric and the cluster of plastics firms connected to it. This reliance was not just on the local market that GE offered (although it was a substantial segment of Marland's market), but also on the feedstock that GE produced, the technical assistance GE often provided to its much smaller neighbor, and the role of GE in the city's apprenticeship programs, which produced skilled workers for the company. After 1974, Ethyl provided most of these services, and so the linkages between the plant and the location were significantly diminished (Nash, 1989).

While labor relations at the plant had traditionally been fairly cooperative and not too adversarial, that began to change, and, as a result of the sales and acquisitions, the workers became increasingly isolated from the plant's owners. Shortly after the second sale in 1976, they unionized and became Local 225 of the International Union of Electronic, Electrical Salaried, Machine and Furniture Workers (IUE). There have been two strikes, one in 1977 (which was a direct result of the company's refusal to negotiate with the new union representation) and one in 1986. But by October 1990, management and the union had agreed to a five-year contract, relations between the union and the management were stable, and problems of the local union were fairly limited compared to many other locals. This was largely because the management at the plant had tended to come from the ranks of workers (Don Madison, the plant's manager, started working in the plant as a machinist in the early 1960s), but also stemmed from the fact that the plant's management was functionally almost as powerless as the workers. That is, the decisions that affected the plant were predominantly made at Tredegar headquarters.

As the recession of the late 1980s and early 1990s intensified, Tredegar Molded began to lay off workers and sell some of its plants (Cuyler, 1992). The layoffs in the Pittsfield plant began in May 1991, and despite having a profitable third quarter in 1991, Tredegar announced on December 2, 1991, that it was seeking to sell the plant in Pittsfield. Tredegar owned a comparable, but nonunion, mold-making plant in Florida and wanted to consolidate its production in that plant. It should be stressed at this point, however, that in 1991, the Pittsfield plant was a profitable one, and the mold-making machines in it were relatively up-to-date. The workers were highly productive and skilled, and the plant was earning money for the company. Tredegar did not wait long to look for a buyer and, in compliance with laws governing plant closures, sent notices to the employees of the Pittsfield plant on January 2, 1992, that it would be closing down in sixty days. The workers, the union, and the town mobilized quickly to begin what would prove to be the protracted process of keeping the plant open.

Mobilizing for the Buyout

A meeting was held at the mayor's office on January 9, 1991, just seven days after the closure announcement and four days into the first term of Pittsfield's mayor Edward Reilly, to discuss the possibilities of keeping the plant open. The idea of a union buyout, which had been entertained by Bob Scott, vice president and treasurer of the IUE's district office, Peter diCicco, president of the IUE's district office, and Mike Surowiec, the local union president, quickly came to the fore.

The most immediate concern for the union was the economic feasibility of the plant, as it would clearly do the workers no good to acquire an unprofitable plant. The union was also concerned about the content of the worker buyout. They believed that employee ownership required employee control, which required a decision-making process and structure that insured that such control was realized (Carleton and Garland, 1993). Bob Scott and Peter diCicco had worked with John Barmack, a private labor consultant and president of Shared Ownership Management Inc. (SOMI) a firm that specializes in negotiating employee buyouts, on several issues before and knew that he shared their views on worker control. Accordingly Barmack was contacted to conduct a quick prefeasibility study on the possible profitability of the plant, and a longer "due diligence" Business Plan to examine the myriad of issues that the worker-owned plant would face. In turn, Barmack contacted the Industrial Cooperatives Association (ICA) to bring them into the project. Together Barmack and the ICA began working on the prefeasibility study. The studies, however, were to cost between $15,000 and $20,000, and the union needed to raise this initial capital before anything else could be done.

Raising this capital was a central component of the meeting at the mayor's office, and the initial impetus for the union to call the mayor to set up the meeting. But the meeting involved many more people than just the union and the mayor. The Central Berkshire Chamber of Commerce, the Pittsfield Department of Economic Development, U.S. Representative John Olver, and the Massachusetts Industrial Services Program (ISP) (a state government agency), all had representatives at the meeting, and would all continue to play a role in the negotiations in the months to come. Importantly, almost all contributed money to do the feasibility studies—including the Chamber of Commerce, in the first time it had become involved in a worker buyout.

With the money having been raised, the mobilization continued along several different lines, as various actors worked to keep the plant open and build political support for its buyout. The most immediately visible form of support came from Pittsfield's local newspaper, the *Berkshire Eagle*, which not only covered the issue closely as the negotiations progressed through 1992, but also wrote several editorials in support of worker ownership, both at Marland Mold in Pittsfield, and more broadly. The *Eagle* wrote its first editorial in support of a worker buyout at Tredegar/Marland on January 8, 1992, the day *before* the meeting at the mayor's office (*Berkshire Eagle*, 1992).

Along with the tone-setting role of the local newspaper, public officials, ranging from the local commissioner of economic development to U.S. Senator Ted Kennedy, mobilized to pressure Tredegar to insure that it was negotiating in good faith. Bob Scott and the IUE also pressured Tredegar to resume sending work orders to the plant in Pittsfield, so it would not close simply by attrition. Because of the political pressure and the efforts of the union, Tredegar agreed to keep the plant open if the workers were planning on buying it, but insisted on receiving a "viable" letter of intent to buy from the union before the March 1 closure date (Cuyler, 1992b).

Negotiating the Buyout

That letter of intent went out in early February 1992. By that point the union's district office had decided that it would use its own money for an equity investment, and a loan had been secured from the First Agriculture Bank of Pittsfield, as the primary sources of capital for the acquisition. The letter of intent, however, was also contingent upon several factors, the principal among them being acquiring further financing for the deal and completing the longer, "due diligence" Business Plan that would examine, in much greater detail than the prefeasibility study, the market potential of the plant, environmental concerns about the site, and several other issues. These concerns notwithstanding, the IUE and Tredegar reached an "agreement in principle" on February 20, 1992 for the company to sell the plant to the union (Cuyler, 1992c).

While this was an important milestone, the bulk of the buyout process still lay ahead. At this point, the vast majority of the negotiations with Tredegar were conducted by Barmack and the ICA, and the role of the union in the process was greatly diminished. The March 1 deadline was now no longer a problem, and Tredegar agreed to continue to send work orders to the plant, but few orders came, probably because Tredegar's customers were concerned about the future of the plant and the company (Carleton and Garland, 1993). As a result, further rounds of layoffs continued to occur as 1992 dragged on.

The lack of work orders highlights several of the key issues that needed to be resolved before the buyout could occur, for while the Pittsfield plant could be profitable based on the labor and machinery there, it still needed to establish a market for itself independent of Tredegar. Also, by selling the plant to its workers rather than closing it, Tredegar was potentially creating a competitor for itself (and this is often one of the primary obstacles faced by workers trying to buy a plant facing closure due to restructuring and consolidations by multiplant firms). The Pittsfield plant had come to depend on Tredegar for its work orders, and its survival as an independent company required not only establishing sales and marketing capacity within the plant, but also creating a customer base to insure the plant had a chance to survive through the first few years of its existence. Getting around this problem required negotiating an agreement with Tredegar over customer lists. This proved to be one of the most difficult components of the negotiation process and required Tredegar to make difficult concessions, as it was consciously closing off marketing avenues to itself. It is unclear why Tredegar was so willing to negotiate so extensively and, as Barmack put it, "I'm not sure die-hard capitalists would have done what they did, because it really wasn't in their best interest."

Other barriers to the buyout remained, however: The first among them was the financing for the project. Barmack and the ICA had secured the principal equity and lending investors, but needed additional sources of capital in the form of loans (not equity investments) to complete the package, and these came from a variety of places, each of which came with its own set of strings and contingencies, which made assembling the financing package the most time-consuming and contentious component of the buyout.

While Barmack and the ICA were negotiating these issues with Tredegar and the myriad of investors and lenders, the IUE and the management were meeting weekly at the plant to educate the workers and the management about the particulars and realities. These meetings were as much for educating the workers as anything else, as Bob Scott worked with the hourly (and also the nonunion salary) workers. These meetings were, as Barmack remembers it, "representative of the workforce and we dealt with issues and educated people (workers and management). Just as workers need help understanding what they can do as owners, they also need to understand what they can't do." These meetings were taking place, however, in the context of an ever-shrinking workforce, as work orders were slow to come in and the buyout negotiations, which should have been completed in April or May, dragged on through the summer. As Mike Surowiec remembers it, "every Wednesday you'd come in here, there'd be less people. It was hard."

In the end, however, the issues were resolved and the final sale of the company occurred on October 2, 1992. It took nine full months of negotiations, but the plant stayed open throughout, and the workers now owned their own firm (via the ESOP). Given the complexity of the negotiation process, the structure of the buyout was comparably elaborate, and was itself the source of much debate.

Structure of the New Firm

The new firm was to be structured as a fairly typical leveraged ESOP, with a trust established that had borrowed the money. The stock distribution plan was, unsurprisingly, a source of great debate, but the plan decided on by Barmack and diCicco distributed an equal block of shares to all workers and then additional shares were based on seniority and salary (Carleton and Garland, 1993). The new company was to be governed by a board of directors, and after much debate it was decided by Barmack, the IUE, and the management that a majority of the board members would be outsiders (not workers or managers from the company).

The board structure decided on was as follows:

2 Hourly workers
1 Salary worker
5 Outside members
    1 Union official
    1 Employee ownership consultant
    1 Financial analyst
    2 Businesspeople
1 President of the company

Corporate Performance

The company has been profitable in the years since the buyout, and has grown dramatically, both in the number of employees and the value of the company's shares. This profitability and growth actually began toward the end of 1992, as the number of work orders, which had been slim through the spring and summer, finally began to pick up. Along with this growth, the plant[8] was making process decisions independently of the confines of a multiplant firm for the first time since it was sold in 1969, and this "local control" (which is how both Mike Surowiec and Don Madison described it) was yielding a more efficient production process and actual profits.

While the number of employees (workers and managers) in the plant had dropped to around thirty during the slowest parts of 1992, its number of employees has more than tripled in the years since then. It should also be stressed that despite discussions by the board of a possible layoff of seven workers during a slow period in 1996 and 1997, the company has never laid off any workers at any time during its existence as a worker-owned firm. While the growth in the number of employees has almost been matched by the growth in the company's sales, it has actually been greatly exceeded by the value of its stock. While the 1990s were clearly a period of substantial growth in the value of publicly traded stocks, those valuations are very different than Marland's. Marland's stock price is legally based on the company's profit, while the valuations of publicly traded stocks are clearly much less closely linked to the economic performance of the companies. Accordingly, its stock has not fallen like almost all the publicly traded stocks have since 2000.

The growth of the company is not only evident from its finances, but has also been a physical process. The company has grown to such an extent that when its neighbor wanted to expand and take over Marland's building, the agreement reached between the two companies allowed Marland to move into a significantly larger, brand-new building in an office park on the edge of town. The opening of the new plant highlights a series of discussions that have taken place on the board of Marland for the last couple of years concerning a possible acquisition of or expansion to a plant, probably outside the U.S. Marland exports between 50 and 60 percent of its molds to non-American plastics companies, and so an overseas plant ("Marland East" was how one of the workers who had been on the board jokingly referred to it) would be economically logical for the company, but it clearly raises some important questions about worker-ownership and place that are important for this project, and which we will return to shortly. Perhaps as important as the corporate performance of Marland, however, are questions of workplace democracy and decision-making. That is, an important measure of the larger scale political implications and meanings of worker-ownership must be whether or not it changes the politics of intrafirm operations.

Workplace Relations and Worker Participation and Control

On the surface, the structure of Marland indicates that there is a participatory decision-making process, and there certainly are many avenues for communication within the company (and these are the reasons why it has been recognized with awards by the national and regional ESOP Associations). The primary example is having three workers on the board of directors out of the total of nine, and having three additional workers sit in on board meetings as observers. Along with the board membership, there are several other mechanisms for communication within the company: 1) monthly meetings take place to discuss manufacturing issues on the shop floor, usually run by the president of the company or the vice-president of manufacturing; 2) bimonthly meetings are held between the union and management to discuss any issues that either party might have; 3) a company newsletter, *Marland Matters*, was created to increase the avenues of communication within the company; 4) the minutes of every board meeting are posted in the cafeteria so all the workers are able to know what occurs on the board; and 5) there are several committees organized and run by the workers to promote discussion of issues of concern. Chief among these is the ESOP committee, which holds activities and events that promote "the culture of employee ownership"—as it was often put by workers at Marland.

Along with the framework of participation, the relationship between the union and management is basically a friendly one at this point. The union holds its meetings inside the company and not in a union hall or another public place in Pittsfield. This is not to say that there isn't conflict between the union and the management, because there certainly is. When I asked the union president if he would lead a strike against himself, he replied, "Absolutely. If you give that up, what have you got left? People always ask me that, 'Why would you strike against yourself? Wouldn't you just be hurting yourself?' And I always say, 'Why would they [the management] let us strike? Wouldn't they be losing their money too?' " When asked if they ever came close to striking, he said, "No. We've never had to."

Worker education is also a central component of the framework that has been constructed at Marland. On the first day of employment, all new workers spend the entire day in an orientation about the company, which is not about the processes involved in mold-making, but instead is about the ESOP "culture" and "philosophy." Similarly, the worker-observers on the board are there to learn how to be board members, and to see how a corporate board operates. ESOP committee members regularly attend regional and national ESOP Association meetings, and go on "company to company" visits to other ESOPs in New England, and Marland has hosted several of these visits by other employee-owners. Finally, workers receive financial training through the State ISP on being an employee-owner, and worker-board members are encouraged to take company-financed correspondence courses in business and finance.

But while the framework for communication is varied, with plenty of outlets, and the company stresses the education of its workers on issues of employee ownership, it was decidedly unclear to me in my conversations with the workers that they had any sense of industrial democracy or control over their own workplace. There are several reasons for this. First, participation rates are very limited, and, according to one hourly worker and past board member, "You have 15 percent, 75 percent, and 10 percent—15 percent believe in it [the ESOP "philosophy], 75 percent don't care, and 10 percent won't believe in it no matter what."[9] The limited participation in the workers' committees was also commented on by another hourly worker, who stated, "One of the big problems here is that the committees are stale, because it's always the same people with the same ideas." And when another worker heard his comment, he concurred and observed, "The majority of the people are not active. The same people are on the different committees, on the union, on everything."

Lack of participation might be a reflection of either passive contentment, or complete alienation from and disgust, with the workplace situation. The workers, taken as a whole, indicated that the former and not the latter contributed to their lack of involvement. When asked if they were satisfied with their workplace, most said they were, and when asked if they could voice a major grievance if they had one, most said they *probably* could (answers were most often in the form of a shrug, and a "I guess so"). The lack of active participation needs to be understood in this light.

Significant questions also remain about the ability of the workers to use their access to the board as a vehicle for worker control. Not only is the majority of the board controlled by people outside the company (which was deliberately done to insure that control of the board did not become too "politicized," in the words of both Barmack and Madison), but worker control through the board is limited in two very important ways. First, management, not the board, controls the operational decisions of the company. That is, all decisions about how work should be organized and structured are the domain of the management. This makes most shop-floor workers skeptical about worker control. One of the past worker board members observed, "They [the other hourlies] can't believe it when I say that operational issues do not concern the board." Second, when I asked former and current hourly workers and board members if they felt like equals with the professionals on the board, the answers were somewhat mixed. Most seemed to feel a bit intimidated at first but said they eventually learned enough to feel comfortable and confident on the board. A current board member was less sanguine, and he responded, "In all honesty, sometimes I wonder. I've had an ongoing argument the last few board meetings, and you wonder if they're listening at all when I bring it up *again*."

Management's control over the daily operations of the company also has clear implications for the prospects of workplace democracy. This control leaves very few avenues for the workers to govern their own work. I asked the union president what an hourly could do if they had a problem with management's decisions about shop-floor operations, and he responded, "They can't go to anybody. They can go to the president of the company and complain, but it won't change anything. The management is able to control operational issues—it's in our union contract, it's everywhere." If a worker has a process improvement idea, then the worker is able to go to the president or vice-president of operations and make the suggestion, which would then be evaluated by the management as to its merits. This occurs fairly regularly, and "process improvements" are actually listed as a regular feature in the company's internal newsletter. But this is clearly not the same as a worker being able to express a grievance about the workplace and have that grievance acted on, and in many ways, these "process improvements" resemble lean production's form of Taylorism (Moody, 1997). The route of last resort for a worker with a complaint would be at the annual shareholders' meeting, where, as one worker put it, "It's the one time a year when you can stand up and people have to hear you." But such demonstrations have rarely occurred, and when asked why not, he responded that, "There's never been a big enough reason."

The outcome of all this is that although the workers might enjoy greater access to management than before, through the various forms of communication discussed above, the power relations within the plant are not fundamentally different than they used to be. Marland has received several awards because of its participatory governance (and this was one of the reasons why I chose the site), but it has been clear that the model of democracy governing the company is one of "consultation" or "placation," to use the language of Arnstein's (1969) famous typology, and not one of a more participatory character. The firm operates in many of the same ways as other firms operating in the capitalist political economy. The goal is profitability, and the only real avenue workers have to assert control over their work and their daily lives hinges on their ability to demonstrate that they can change the process to make it more profitable.

The Potential and Limits of Collective Ownership of Work

Several conclusions can be drawn from this chapter. First, worker ownership is viable and can flourish as a segment within the capitalist economy. While the number of worker-cooperatives has not grown much in recent years, ESOPs have grown significantly since 1974, and that growth continues despite legal changes in 1996 that made ESOPs less appealing to large, publicly traded firms. This viability, however, can be limited by the time and capital needed for workers to acquire their worksite. Marland's acquisition was a lengthy process that spanned almost an entire year—and this was a case where the process *should* have gone smoothly since the company was willing to sell the plant, and the bulk of the capital was raised fairly early in the process. The difficulty encountered during the Marland buyout clearly illustrates the barriers to worker-ownership.

Worker-owned firms are more profitable than their traditionally owned competitors, and their viability is more clearly demonstrated by their profitability than by their growth. In Marland, the workers and management attributed the increased profitability of the plant to several factors. First, the plant's management has been able to absorb the functions of sales and marketing for the first time since the plant was initially bought in 1969. Second, the workers have been able to generate process improvements that have sped up the ability of the plant to handle work orders. Third, the largely external board has played an important role in working with the management to construct long-term goals and the capacity to meet them. Worker-owned firms, however, clearly exist in the market and can fail in just the same ways that traditionally owned firms do—as is demonstrated by closure of CHCB, which resulted from its inability to diversify when the market changed.

Second, worker-ownership is a framework that can be used to improve the lives of the workers involved. A national survey analyzing the employee benefits in ESOPs relative to their traditionally owned competitors found that ESOPs paid hourly wages of 5 to 12 percent more than their competitors, and retirement benefits for ESOPs averaged almost three times their competitors (Employee Ownership Report, 1998). Most of these benefits, however, are tied to the ESOPs themselves, so they are more vulnerable than other retirement benefits that are more diversified.[10] In the case of Marland Mold, the workers clearly felt an improvement in their lives since the alternative was unemployment, and the very real possibility of that condition being long-term. As one of the workers put it, "We had no idea where this was going to go. We didn't have any vision for this far down the road. We were trying to save our jobs. We were all in our forties and fifties, and we needed these jobs." Beyond the lack of alternatives, the workers at Marland seem genuinely content with their place of employment. They feel that they have good jobs that pay well and that they are going to be able to retire well since their shares have appreciated so dramatically. Similarly, given that the overwhelming majority of the worker-owners at CHCA and its affiliates had previously been on public assistance, there is clearly a significant improvement in their lives.

The results become more mixed, however, when the issue turns to the relationships between worker-ownership and the locality in which that ownership is realized. The first half of the equation—from locality to workplace—was clearly apparent in the mobilization and negotiation of Marland's worker buyout. The role of place-dependent institutions like the municipal government, the local Chamber of Commerce, the daily newspaper, the local bank, and the area's representative in Washington, was strongly evident, since they all played important roles in making the buyout a reality. Similarly, while, in its inception, CHCA received support from national-scale organizations like the ICA Group, the driving force behind it was CSS, a definitively local organization.

The second half of the equation—from workplace to locality—is more ambiguous. It is unclear how much worker-ownership impacts other workers in other firms in the same localities. Marland's forward and backward linkages continued to be extralocal in scale, and so its remaining open is likely to have had little impacts on other firms in Pittsfield. And while the CHCA has played a very proactive role in promoting worker-ownership, it has done so sectorally rather than locally—all of its affiliates are well beyond the South Bronx or even the New York metropolitan area. Further, Marland has also been seriously discussing opening another plant, which would not only not be in Pittsfield, but probably not even in the United States. What is most troubling about this is not only that it runs the risk of recreating the very process of capital mobility and disinvestment that were the source of the problem in the first place, but since Marland's decision-making process is fairly undemocratic, the second plant could be constructed without much of a discussion about its implications.

But the lack of economic impacts does not mean that the buyout hasn't transformed the city in any way. The very public buyout process (as a result of the *Eagle*'s coverage and its many editorials promoting worker-ownership) brought with it a new set of understandings to the city of Pittsfield. As one Marland worker put it, "We put a lot of things out there, on the table. What we did was unknown to most people. Now we have local politicians who look at this as a potential solution to a problem." And it wasn't just bravado talking, for when GE Plastics announced in 1998 that it was going to close its last remaining plant in and around the city (most of the others were closed in the 1980s—see Nash, 1989), the reaction of the workers at that plant was to get in touch with Don Madison, who began to meet regularly with the workers and management there, and brought the ICA into the process as well.[11]

Finally, while the linkages from workplace to locality are ambiguous and rather tenuous, the connections between worker-ownership and local autonomy might be even thinner. Two of the primary local institutions that were part of Marland's buyout process would, in all likelihood, not play those roles again. The *Berkshire Eagle*, which had been a family-owned newspaper for several generations, was bought in 1995 by MediaNews Group, a national firm famous for buying, and gutting, small newspapers (Simurda, 1995), and Mark Miller the editor was fired. The First Agriculture Bank, whose president had been quoted in the *Eagle* as saying, "We are the largest commercial lender in the county and we make our banking decisions locally" (Cuyler, 1992g), and which had been an important source of the financing of the deal (and sat through many hours of negotiation with Tredegar), was bought in 1993 by the Bank of Boston (which would then go on to merge with BayBank and then Fleet Bank). And so while the buyout might have sheltered the workers of Marland from the impacts of larger scale restructuring, the relationships that make up the locality are so varied and complex that transforming one of them, in isolation from other changes, is not likely to significantly alter the relations of power and control. This is, admittedly, a high standard for this buyout to meet, and clearly one victory and two losses is preferable to three losses.

But the prospects for transforming the meanings of work, property, and ownership has also demonstrated itself to be being rather mixed. CHCA, which was created through the efforts of CSS, was deliberately constructed as a cooperative because of an inherent critique of the structures and practices of an exploitative industry. The situation at Marland Mold, however, is very different. The workers, management, and board of Marland have largely accepted the dominant meanings of work and corporate self-interest. The very fact that there has been serious discussion given to acquiring another plant, and becoming a multiplant firm indicates that the management and workers have not used their experiences of near plant closure and unemployment, due to their existence within such a firm, to generate a critique of the larger structures and processes that had resulted in their need to buyout the plant in the first place. The Marland buyout was born of crisis, but now that the crisis has long since subsided, the firm has become, for all intents and purposes, just another company—albeit a particularly benevolent one. The model of worker-ownership at Marland seems largely one of self-interest and "bootstrappism," but with that logic simply moved up a scale from the individual to the collective. As the Cooperative Healthcare Network demonstrates, worker-ownership need not mean this, and instead can be an important part of a much more radical political project, but in the rather "typical" case of Marland, this is how it has manifested itself. Absent political connections able to interpret worker-ownership differently, this is likely to continue to be the case at Marland and elsewhere.

CHAPTER 4

Collective Ownership of Housing

In response to the recognized injustices of the private real-estate market, and in particular, the "choices" of disinvestment or gentrification, several different kinds of organizations are working toward the goal of transforming housing and property from commodities to collectively owned social goods. Limited-Equity Cooperatives, Mutual Housing Associations (MHAs), and Community Land Trusts are the most common forms of collective control over housing and land. This chapter begins with a short discussion of the re-emergence of gentrification and the lack of affordable housing in American cities. It then describes the different forms of collective ownership of housing created in American communities. Included in these descriptions are two short case studies of a community land trust and limited-equity housing cooperatives. This will be followed by a much more detailed case study of the Mutual Housing Association of Southwestern Connecticut (MHASWC). While the MHASWC is a regional organization, the case study primarily focuses on the association's two oldest developments, the residents therein, and the impacts of Mutual Housing on the West Side neighborhood of Stamford, Connecticut. The chapter concludes by discussing the potential and limits of forms of collective ownership of housing and land.

Gentrification and the Crisis of Affordable Housing in America

Among the many economic changes of the last twenty-five years, there has been a dramatic transformation in some inner-city neighborhoods with regards to the flows of investment capital available for housing construction and rehabilitation. The period from the end of World War II has often been described as one of suburbanization and the continuing decline of inner-city neighborhoods (see Beauregard, 1993, for an excellent discussion of the images associated with these processes). In the last quarter century, however, a powerful counter-trend has emerged in many places, as inner-city neighborhoods have become destinations for capital investment in the real-estate market. This counter-trend of gentrification should be understood as emerging directly out of the suburbanization process, as its (suburbanization's) long-term disinvestment in inner-city areas created the potential for profitable reinvestment in some of those very same disinvested-in areas (see Smith, 1979). Disinvestment and gentrification are therefore not different processes, but two different expressions of the same flows of capital investment in real-estate development. The problem with gentrification is that it has rarely manifested itself in forms that improve the quality of life for those that had been living there during the period of disinvestment. Instead it has usually displaced those low-income residents from their homes (Smith and Williams, 1986; Smith, 1996).

Thus inner-city reinvestment in the form of gentrification locally intensifies the growing crisis of housing affordability in the United States. There is a housing affordability crisis in this country, and it became significantly worse over the course of the last decade. This reality is fairly well known, and it therefore does not require much discussion here. A few simple data should suffice in making this clear.[1] For instance, the Department of Housing and Urban Development found that the number of households with "worst case housing needs"[2] grew by more than 600,000 from 1991 to 1997, and was more than 5.4 million households (or 12.3 million people) by the end of that period (U.S. Department of Housing and Urban Development, 2000, p. 13). This, however, is only a fraction of the 13.7 million households nationwide, or *one in every seven households*, that face "critical housing needs"[3] (Stegman, Quercia, and McCarthy, 2000, p. 6). These affordability problems are not simply felt by the poorest of the poor, or the permanently unemployed; of those 13.7 million households, more than 3 million are in moderate-income working families (Stegman, Quercia, and McCarthy, 2000, p. 7). Finally, the amount of housing affordable to low- and very low–income households plummeted in the last decade, and just in the short time "between 1993 and 1995, the number of unsubsidized units affordable to very low-income households was down 8.6 percent—*a decrease of nearly 900,000 units*" (The State of Affordable Housing, 2000, emphasis added).

This crisis in housing affordability is extremely important and deserves attention in and of itself. But this affordability crisis was far from uniformly experienced, however; nationally, rental costs grew much more rapidly in inner cities than in the suburbs in the 1990s (U.S. Department of

Housing and Urban Development, 2000a, p 55). This fact, and a large number of local case studies (see, for instance: Coalition for a Livable Future, 1999; Hackworth, 2000; Hall, 2000; Harvey, et al., 2000; Martinson, 2000; Priluck, 2000; Smith and DeFilippis, 1999; Wyly and Hammel, 1999; Yee and Quiroz-Martinez, 1999) demonstrate that gentrification, and its accompanying displacement of low-income residents, powerfully reemerged after its temporary retreat during the recession of the early 1990s.

Gentrification is complexly interconnected with the processes of deindustrialization, the growth of the Finance, Insurance and Real Estate (FIRE) sectors and their employment, and the increasing interconnections between real estate and other forms of investment capital (see Hamnett, 2000, for a good discussion of these connections). It is thus both a product and producer of capital mobility and globalization. It has also fundamentally reshaped how inner-city development needs to be conceptualized.

Since the emergence of gentrification, it has become untenable to argue that reinvestment is a desirable end in-and-of-itself for low-income people and residents of disinvested areas. Instead, rightfully conceived, reinvestment needs to be understood through the lens of questions such as: What kind of investment? For whom? Controlled by whom? These processes have left residents of low-income neighborhoods in a situation where, since they exert little control over either investment capital or their homes, they are facing the "choices" of either continued disinvestment and decline in the quality of the homes they live in, or reinvestment that results in their displacement. The importance of gentrification, therefore, is that it clearly demonstrates that low-income people, and the neighborhoods they live in, suffer not from a lack of capital but from a lack of power and control over even the most basic components of life—that is, the places called home. In order to realize that power, communities have created forms of ownership in which investment decisions are made collectively, and it is to these that this chapter now turns.

Limited Equity Housing Cooperatives

Housing cooperatives have been part of the American housing stock for well over 100 years. And some feminists and socialists in the nineteenth century argued that collectively owning housing was just as important in a transformed society as was workers owning the means of production (see Stone, 1993). The early cooperatives, however, were luxury developments called "home clubs" which prided themselves on their exclusivity (Siegler and Levy, n.d.). It wasn't until the twentieth century that cooperatives became more politically and socially progressive in their motivations, and in the interwar period, many union-built cooperatives were constructed in the U.S.—with the bulk of them being in New York City. With the support of public policies, including tax breaks on property value appreciations and direct subsidies, cooperatives have become a significant, if still rather peripheral, part of American housing. There are more than 1.5 million cooperative housing units in the U.S., and cooperatives are by far the largest form of collectively owned and controlled housing in the United States. Most of these, however, are market-rate or luxury cooperatives with little social or political goal or mission.

But this is certainly not true for all cooperatives, and there are about 400,000 housing units in limited-equity co-ops nationwide (PolicyLink, 2002). This figure is a bit misleading, since they are highly geographically concentrated, with the absolute majority of these located in New York City (Rae, 1997). The number of co-ops grew dramatically and very rapidly through the 1970s, as part of the self-help housing that emerged in this period as a result of the disinvestment and abandonment in many inner-city areas (see Kolodny, 1987). This was particularly true in New York City, where abandonment led to a substantial stock of city-owned housing that was often converted by the tenants into limited-equity co-ops (see Leavitt and Saegert, 1990; Rae, 1997).

A housing cooperative is similar to other forms of homeownership in that the resident is not just a tenant but also an owner, and therefore possesses a set of rights and responsibilities. That, however, is where the similarities end. And what residents own is not their housing unit, but a share in the corporation that owns the housing complex.[4] The corporation owns and controls the housing development, and the residents are the shareholders of the corporation. What distinguishes limited equity from other, more commonly found, co-ops is that the price of the owners' shares is not determined by the larger real-estate market (as it is for most co-ops), but by a set formula determined by the particular cooperative's bylaws and subscription agreements. Those bylaws restrict the resale price of the cooperative shares, and thus limit the households' equity, in order to guarantee the permanent affordability of the housing units in the cooperative. The extent to which equity is limited ranges from zero-equity agreements, in which resident-shareholders receive back what they initially put in when they decide to leave the cooperative, to agreements that allow for some price inflation and a return on any additional investments that might have been made. While such equity restrictions are legally enforceable if written into the governing by-laws of the cooperative, there is always the real possibility of the cooperative members themselves dissolving the coop or lifting the equity restrictions. In order to guard against this possibility, and insure that the long-term interests of the community do not get displaced by the interests of the current resident-shareholders, third-party agreements are often part of the conversion of a rental building to a limited-equity co-op. This can either be with a government agency subsidizing the co-op, a community organization, or sometimes a community land trust.

Turning Squatters into Owners: The Case of the Lower East Side Limited-Equity Co-ops

In one of the most visible neighborhoods where capital disinvestment had led to abandonment and squatting in the abandoned buildings, the long-running dispute between the Lower East Side of Manhattan squatters and New York City's government has finally come to an end—with the squatters converting the properties into limited-equity housing cooperatives. The Lower East Side has a long history of poverty and immigration, which itself has a long history of being romanticized and (variously successfully and unsuccessfully) sanitized, commodified, and gentrified by artists, middle-class people, and real-estate developers (see Mele, 2000; Smith, 1996; Smith and DeFilippis, 1999, for discussions of this). In this mix, and in the widespread disinvestments and decay of the area, squatting emerged in the 1970s. The squats, which, as groups, exemplified the class, race, and cultural diversity of the area, became a visible sign of both the poverty of the area and the almost utopian political visions of many of the area's artists and activists. But the squats were also in almost constant conflict with the police and the city government, and this conflict was most visceral during the police riots in Tompkins Square Park in 1988, when the squatters joined with a broad base of community and antigentrification activists to fight the police over control of the park. The fights with the police and city government continued through the 1990s, as successive city governments tried to forcibly evict the squatters from their city-owned homes. Increasingly in the 1990s, however, many of the squats also came into conflict with the area's CDCs—which wanted the properties to construct affordable housing and which came to view many of the squatters as middle-class white kids "slumming" for the romance of it.[5]

Beginning in 1999, many of the squats began discussions with the Urban Homesteading Assistance Board (UHAB) to convert the buildings to limited-equity housing cooperatives. UHAB, which had been founded in 1973, has a long history of working with tenants to create and manage tenant cooperatives. UHAB, in turn, began conversations with the city about turning over the properties to the squatters. By the summer of 2001, an agreement was reached between the squatters, UHAB, and the city. UHAB bought the "vacant" buildings from the city (for $1, as is common for city government practice), and then turned the buildings over to the squatters. Each squatter put in $250 for his or her share in their corpora-tion (the eleven buildings are separate corporations), and their resale is capped at between $6,000 and $9,000, depending on the unit's size—and the resale is even more tightly constrained for the first two years. Not all of the squatters or squats agreed to this conversion, however, and one of the major squats in the area has continued its existence as such.

Community Land Trusts

The community land trust (CLT) "model" was created in the late 1960s by civil-rights activists concerned about the declines in black property own-ership in the south. These concerns led to the creation of the Institute for Community Economics in Massachusetts (Institute for Community Eco-nomics, 1982; Orvis, 1998). As its origins would suggest, the model was originally constructed as a rural preservation model designed to protect farmers from creeping and speculative development, or foreclosure of family farms by hostile financial institutions. Since the early 1980s, it has been imported into urban areas to protect affordable housing from creep-ing and speculative development or the abandonment of affordable hous-ing by hostile landlords and financial institutions. There are 86 CLTs already operating in the United States, and there are an additional 32 in the process of being created. Collectively these contain about 5,500 units of housing, in which almost three-fourths of residents earn less than half of their area's median income (DeFilippis, 2002). A disproportionate number of these are in the northeast, and New England in particular. It should also be stated that the CLT model's recent growth has largely been in areas of rapid economic growth in the 1990s—the San Francisco Bay area and the Pacific Northwest, where antisprawl measures and large in-migrations of high-paid labor have made land values and housing affordability substan-tial issues.

In a CLT, a community organization owns and manages the land, while the residents "own" (sometimes cooperatively through either an MHA or a limited-equity cooperative, sometimes individually, sometimes even as af-fordable rental units) only the housing units located on the land. The cen-tral feature of land trusts is the separation of buildings from the land they are upon. The individuals "own" the housing by virtue of long-term (usu-ally 99 years, with inheritance rights) ground leases that they sign with the organization keeping the land in trust. The housing costs paid by residents vary from CLT to CLT, but in all cases there are strict limitations on hous-ing costs and the resale price that can be sought by resident "owners" when they choose to leave. Additionally, CLTs always possess the right of first re-fusal when a unit is to be sold. The argument is simply that people should collect on any investments they make in the units, but any further appreciation in the housing value is socially created and therefore does not belong to the individual.

The governing boards of CLTs are usually comprised as follows: one-third leaseholders (residents); one-third nonresident community members, one-third public officials. CLTs thus limit resident control (relative to MHAs or limited-equity co-ops), and emphasize community and public control—and this reflects the understanding of the communal nature of land that runs through what land trusts do.

Burlington Community Land Trust

Through a grassroots effort, and with little money, in 1981 Bernie Sanders became the mayor of Burlington, Vermont. At the core of the coalition of groups that brought him to power were affordable-housing advocates, and, accordingly, housing affordability was a central plank in the set of policies he was able to implement in his time as mayor (for excellent discussions of the experiences of the Burlington progressives see, Clavel, 1986; Conroy, 1990). And Burlington needed it, too. At the time of his inauguration, a series of factors (including the growth of the University of Vermont, a rapidly growing regional economy, and a redeveloped downtown) had all combined to make housing costs increasingly prohibitively expensive. By the early 1980s, housing prices in Burlington—both renter- and owner-occupied—were growing about twice as fast as average incomes in the city (Davis, 1994, p. 166). It was in this context that the newly progressive local government began to look at ways to construct and maintain permanently affordable housing. And in 1984 the Burlington Community Land Trust was incorporated. This incorporation was, in part, driven by the city government, principally working through its Community and Economic Development Office (CEDO), which had received $200,000 in 1983 to create a citywide land trust. As the Burlington CLT grew over the years, its support from the city government (and CEDO in particular) continued to play a major part in that growth. CEDO continued to disburse money to the CLT, often in the form of federal Community Development Block Grant (CDBG) funds, but also through more creative sources, such as the Burlington Employees Retirement System (the municipal workers' pension fund, which created a line of credit for the CLT in the late 1980s).

Thus the CLT, which was originally established to work principally in the "Old North End"—the working-class neighborhood just north of downtown Burlington (which faced particular gentrification pressures due to its proximity to downtown and Lake Champlain)—grew into a citywide

CLT. Currently its portfolio is both large and diverse, and it has become one of the models of the CLT movement nationwide. The land trust now has about 500 units of housing on its land. About half of these are owner-occupied, and half are rental or mutual housing. It also has a set of community centers and facilities that are on its land, as well as a family emergency shelter, special needs housing (for homeless women and people with HIV or AIDS), and single-room-occupancy (SRO) housing for single people with very low incomes.

The CLT has a twelve-person board, with the standard board structure of one-third leaseholders, one-third representatives from community organizations, and one-third at-large community members. Its board is elected by its membership, which consists of all leaseholders (who are automatically members), and anyone else from the community who pays the $1 membership fee.

Mutual Housing Associations

A Mutual Housing Association is similar to a large-scale limited-equity housing cooperative, although it differs from most co-ops in that the residents do not own shares in the cooperative of their residence (which could then be resold when they move). Instead, the housing is off the market entirely, and ownership of it is permanently in the hands of the Association. Residents rent their units from the Association but, at the same time, the residents constitute the Association. The model is therefore substantially different from housing produced in either the for-profit real-estate market, or the not-for-profit CDC sector. While MHAs are similar in some respects to CDCs (primarily in that they build affordable housing for low-income people), they differ in two basic ways. First, while most CDCs advocate traditional forms of land and housing tenure, albeit more affordably, MHAs reject these, and instead promote and implement a form of mixed-ownership with individuals and communities possessing different components of the rights, interests, and responsibilities of ownership. Second, while many CDCs are participatory in character, and understand organizing to be an integral part of what they do, many others do not. Conversely, community and resident participation is written into the governance structures of MHAs, which, accordingly, stress this component of their development work.

MHAs are expansionist organizations, having the explicit goal of taking more and more housing out of the private market and moving it into collective ownership (which further distinguishes them from most limited-equity housing cooperatives, since they are largely stand-alone entities). There are two reasons for this. First, since they believe in the model of mixed collective/individual ownership, they want to bring more units into this framework. Second, the greater the number of units owned and controlled by the groups, the greater the economies of scale realized by the organizations in the maintenance and management of the properties, and the greater the possibility of realizing their goal of fiscal self-sufficiency. Costs for MHAs are front-ended in the acquisition process, making the units more affordable and the organizations more fiscally viable over the long term. Finally, the collective ownership is structured so that the units are permanently taken off the private housing market.

History

Mutual housing associations (MHAs) emerged in the early 1980s from two different sources. First, they were based on the model of housing cooperatives prevalent in continental Europe from the mid-nineteenth century, but particularly in the period after World War II. The principal European influence on American MHAs came from the experience of German mutual housing (Barnes, 1982; see also Boelhouwer and van der Heijden, 1998). Mutual housing is an established component of the housing sector in Germany, and in the period from 1949 to 1971, over 4.4 million units of mutual housing were produced in West Germany—one-third of the total housing constructed over that period (Peterman and Young, 1991, p 30). Second, MHAs also have their roots in the history of American limited-equity housing cooperatives.

Despite the importance of the mutual housing model in Europe, it was not until the late 1970s that it began to receive attention in the United States. The initial impetus came from the newly formed Neighborhood Reinvestment Corporation (NRC) to investigate the possibility of establishing the model within the US. The NRC had been created by Congress with the Housing and Community Development Act of 1978, and began the first MHA demonstration project in Baltimore in 1982. In the years since then, the number of MHAs has grown, and there are at least thirty operating in the United States (Krinsky and Hovde, 1996, Taylor, 1997; Neighborhood Reinvestment Corporation, 2001). This growth, however, primarily took place through the 1980s, and the number of MHAs has rather stagnated since the early 1990s. About 46 percent of the residents of MHAs live on less than 50 percent of their area's median income, and another 41 percent earn between 50 and 80 percent of their area's median (Taylor, 1997). So MHAs tend to serve a low- to very low–income population.

Structure and Capitalization

In MHAs, the residents pay monthly housing charges to the Association, which can either be fixed, with periodic adjustments just to keep pace with inflation, or are paid by the residents as a percentage of the residents' incomes (between 26 and 29 percent). In either payment system, the logic that determines the cost of the housing is not the market, but the agreed policies of the MHA. Residents also contribute to the financing of their units and buildings by performing mandatory maintenance work, often as much as ten hours a month. Along with their monthly housing charges and maintenance work, in most MHAs residents must also pay a one-time membership fee ranging from around one thousand to several thousand dollars, which is used to help capitalize the Associations. This fee earns interest, is refundable when the resident leaves the Association, and is often viewed by residents and staff alike as an initial, if limited, form of equity. Residents who can't afford this initial investment are able to borrow the money from their Association, and pay it back over an extended period of time.

MHAs are principally capitalized through grants, low-interest loans, and development fees. Acquisition and construction costs tend to be paid for through a combination of grants from the public sector at any or all scales (with the NRC providing grants to many MHAs), loans from private investors (often to receive a Low Income Housing Tax Credit or, for banks, to fulfill Community Reinvestment Act obligations), and subsidized loans from the public sector, and, to a limited extent, equity investments from private or public investors. Association ownership of the units means that the affordability subsidies required for acquisition do not get lost over time, as they do in most HUD-subsidized housing (like project-based Section 8) as units revert back to market price when affordability restrictions expire (see Bach, 1999).[6] Instead, the units are permanently taken off the private housing market, and therefore rendered perpetually affordable. It is this attribute of MHAs (which it largely shares with CLTs and limited-equity co-ops), perhaps more than any other, that allows them to be one of the most fiscally frugal (over the long term) forms of affordable housing construction and management. Operation costs are financed primarily through the development fees and management fees (the "carrying charges" paid by residents) which MHAs receive for building and managing their housing. Operational support grants from the public sector are also an important part of the financing of the operations of MHAs.

While MHAs are often not significantly different in practice from participatory CDCs, unlike CDCs, MHAs have a structure that insures resident participation and, theoretically, control. The NRC's standard board structure, which most MHAs have adopted, is that residents and residents-in-waiting make up the majority of the board of directors, with the remaining seats being taken by the associations' staffs and by representatives from local government, businesses, and nongovernment organizations.

The associations are controlled by their boards, on which residents maintain majorities.

The Mutual Housing Association of Southwestern Connecticut
Fairfield County, Stamford, and the West Side

Fairfield County is one of the most affluent counties in the United States, and has functioned primarily as a set of suburban residential communities for commuters to New York City and into downtown Stamford. While Fairfield County consists primarily of affluent bedroom communities, Stamford has been both an affluent suburb and a city in its own right. The early history of Stamford is dominated by shipping and the industrial activities associated with trade and port facilities. By the mid-1960s, however, the city was experiencing deindustrialization, and downtown Stamford was a site of disinvestment, an ensemble of closed factories and low-income housing.

The town began a massive urban renewal project in the mid-1960s. The plan required the demolition of all the housing in the downtown and the relocation of the residents therein. The relocation never really occurred on a large scale, and there has been a real shortage of affordable housing in Stamford since this time. Urban renewal in Stamford was also driven by the city's ability to attract large companies to move their headquarters from New York City. The first to move, GTE, left New York City for Stamford in 1970 (Frey, 1991). The process grew from that starting point, and by the mid-1980s, Stamford was being hailed as having been completely "reborn" as a city of corporate headquarters and the white-collar workers associated with those headquarters (Klein, 1986). By 1996, the area was rated by *Sales and Marketing Management Magazine* as having the highest median "Effective Buying Income" in the country (Conlon, 1996).

This period of economic growth for Stamford has been mirrored by comparable increases in the cost of living. According to the National Low Income Housing Coalition, in 2001 the Stamford MSA had the third highest rent in the country—behind only San Francisco and San Jose, California (*Out of Reach*, 2001). Also, despite this period of growth, significant portions of the city of Stamford have not seen their lives improved. In particular, the West Side of Stamford has a long history of disinvestment and decay.

The neighborhood is immediately adjacent to downtown, separated only by the Mill River (see Figure 4.1). It has a long history of being a destination for immigrant workers, beginning with the Irish who settled in the area in the mid-1800s. The area went through a period of disinvestment

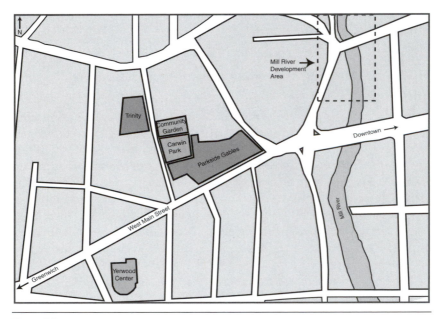

Figure 4.1

and decline in the post-war era that mirrored many inner-city neighborhoods throughout the country, but it was a relatively modest one, as the area retained a level of stability over the years. The worst period of decline, the 1970s, only saw a population loss of 13 percent (Department of Neighborhood Planning, 1985).

The 1980s was a period of modest investment in the area, as it began to face some gentrification pressures, due largely to its proximity to downtown. These pressures continued through the 1990s and new, relatively affluent workers moved to the area, raising the area's mean household income to $42,250 in 1997, although the median remained much lower at $32,189— thus reflecting the discrepancy between the different classes of residents (Byrne, McKinney & Associates, 1997). The area's housing stock is overwhelmingly renter-occupied, and the West Side, and Stamford as a whole, also possesses a very tight housing market, with a less-than 4-percent vacancy rate for rental units citywide and in the neighborhood itself (Bureau of the Census, 2000). Together, these leave the residents particularly vulnerable to the threat of displacement from gentrification. This then is the context in which Mutual Housing emerged in Stamford and in particular in the West Side.

History

The Mutual Housing Association of Southwestern Connecticut was incorporated in 1990 as a not-for-profit, tax-exempt organization. It is headquartered near downtown Stamford, but its first two developments were built in the West Side, and the neighborhood remains the central focus of the Association's work. While the Association is regional in its orientation and operates a total of four mutual housing developments in Fairfield County, this case study is about its two developments in the West Side.

The early history of the organization is one of political organizing rather than housing construction. It began in 1987, well before the November 1991 opening of its first housing development of Parkside Gables. The initial impetus for the creation of the MHA came from the NRC, which issued a Request for Proposals (RFP) for cities to sponsor an MHA. Stamford Neighborhood Housing Services (NHS), a local not-for-profit developer of affordable housing, had been acquiring some abandoned properties on the north side of West Main Street in Stamford's West Side. NHS's original plan was to build affordable rental units on the properties, but when the NRC issued the RFP, NHS, which was an affiliate of the NRC's national "NeighborhoodWorks" network, decided to develop mutual housing (Smith, 1999).

After Stamford won the bid for the MHA, the NRC, as is its standard practice, hired an organizer to generate support for mutual housing within the community and to work with potential future residents. The method that was used to generate support within the community was a "straight organizing process" (Ondrocik, 1999). Ms. Ondrocik started by meeting with community leaders—both formally and informally recognized, including people from local churches and church groups, neighborhood associations, city government, and local business leaders. In this process, Ms. Ondrocik created a framework in which more than 100 people in Stamford were actively involved (Wood, 1999), and in which more than 500 different people, in total, participated in public meetings, city council hearings, zoning board meetings, and information sessions (Connecticut Housing Coalition, 1998).

Along with the public hearings, Ms. Ondrocik set up a group of committees of interested community members and potential residents to oversee the development of Parkside Gables. These committees dealt with every step in the planning process—including the design of the new housing development, the resident selection process, and the bylaws that would govern the housing. These committee meetings took up the better part of the two years planning for and designing the development. Thus, even before the housing had been constructed, its future residents, and the community as a whole, were exercising control over the development.

Parkside Gables opened in November 1991 as the first housing development of the MHASWC. It is a two-story town-house development. Each unit has its own driveway and garage, and in many ways it resembles a suburban development project (Figure 4.2). The development is constructed

Figure 4.2

into a set of miniblocks, that run inward from West Main Street. Access to the development is not tightly controlled, and people can enter and exit it freely. Less than a block away from Parkside Gables lies Trinity Park apartments, the second development project of the MHASWC (Figure 4.1). This building, originally built to house Stamford residents who needed to be relocated due to the urban renewal of the 1960s, had fallen into disrepair and had suffered from long-term disinvestment by its landlord. The building was condemned in 1992 by the Stamford Health Department (Houriet, 1993), and was thereafter acquired by Mutual Housing. The rehabbing of Trinity Park began in 1993, and the building was reopened as mutual housing in 1996 (Figure 4.3), with many of its former residents returning to their newly rehabbed homes.

Along with housing production, Mutual Housing has been involved, directly or indirectly, with several other community groups and people organizing in the West Side, and the association has engaged in the ongoing, and ever-contested, process of producing the place that it is in. The role of MH in the neighborhood began early in the 1990s, with the establishment, by several MH residents, of the group West Side United Neighbors (or WestSUN, as it is commonly known). Residents in WestSUN, along with other West Side residents, began a neighborhood crime watch in 1993. Mutual housing residents have also been active in other endeavors that have transformed their neighborhood. Parkside and Trinity are separated by Carwin Park (Figure 4.1), a city park that had been used primarily as a

Figure 4.3

site for drug dealers and had limited equipment for children to play with. The residents of Mutual Housing organized to get the city of Stamford to renovate the park in the early 1990s, and it has become one of the focal points of the neighborhood, as it hosts the neighborhood's annual picnic in July. Adjacent to the park was a vacant lot, which through the early to mid-1990s was transformed into a community garden by Mutual Housing residents and other residents from the area. Also, the indoor swimming pool at the publicly owned Yerwood Center, which had been closed since the mid-1980s, was renovated and reopened in 1996 largely in response to political pressure from the residents of Mutual Housing (Shen, 1996).

The most significant role that Mutual Housing residents have played in the place-making process in the West Side has been to take the lead in getting residents involved in the City's plan to develop the Mill River corridor (which separates downtown Stamford from the West Side). This plan, originally driven by the city government, has been transformed into a plan for the West Side, and Mutual Housing has worked with residents to generate a comprehensive community plan for the area, instead of relying on the city's development goals. The plan, which calls for the construction of affordable housing, parks and recreation areas (like basketball courts), and a pedestrian bridge connecting the West Side with downtown, conflicts with the vision expressed by the City's Urban Renewal Commission, which has spearheaded the project. As of the time of this writing, the political struggle surrounding the future of this space is still unresolved, but at the very least, the West Side residents are organized around a coherent view of development and the place of their community as they engage in this struggle.

Structure and Governance

The Mutual Housing Association of Southwestern Connecticut is a member-based organization. Five types of members (Resident, Resident-in-Waiting, Corporate Sector, Public Sector, Nonprofit Sector) have voting rights, but the residents comprise the vast majority of its members. Voting rights, which include selecting the Association's board of directors, are formally exercised only at the annual meeting or at special meetings that might be called to deal with a particular issue or conflict, but these have rarely been called. The board of directors, which governs the Association, meets monthly and consists of 21 members, apportioned by membership type as follows:

10 Resident members
1 Waiting-resident member
2 Government-sector members
4 Corporate-sector members
2 Nonprofit-sector members
1 NHS representative
1 At-large member (from either government, corporate, or nonprofit)

Along with the board of directors, the Association has a staff that handles the daily work of managing the housing, and also includes resident organizing—although previously there were two resident organizers on staff in Stamford, there currently is only one.

The residents role in decision-making within the Association is not limited to their involvement on the board of directors but also includes resident councils, the first level of recourse for other residents who have problems with their units or have other concerns (safety, neighbors, etc.) that need to be addressed.

Along with the initial committees that Ms. Ondorcik established in the organizing stage of the development, a set of other *resident* committees was created to govern the development once it was approaching completion. These committees, however, dwindled over the years, and so did the overall role of the residents in governing their housing. Organizing is an ongoing process, but by the mid-1990s, as the Association focused on new developments elsewhere, the organizing component of the Association was given less of a priority and therefore foundered. Since a change in leadership in 1998, there has been a renewed effort to reinvigorate the resident councils and to place control of the housing more firmly in the hands of residents via these councils.

The question of residents' control over the governance of the Association was a major issue addressed in a survey I conducted of the residents in Parkside and Trinity Park. When asked how much influence they felt they had over the decisions made in Mutual Housing, they responded as follows:

Table 4.1 Resident Sense of Control in Mutual Housing

	Frequency	Percent
A lot of influence	21	26.6
Some influence	26	32.9
A little influence	6	7.6
Hardly any influence	17	21.5
Don't know	9	11.4

While most residents feel they have at least some influence in decision-making, they do not indicate a situation or a perception of complete resident control (Table 4.1). The sense of resident involvement and control has decreased over time, as expressed by an original resident in Parkside Gables who said, "Well, when we first moved in, we thought we were going to that ownership level, but we never got there. We haven't got out of it what we thought we would get out of it. If you look at all the things they are doing now . . . if you had been here [in 1994], they had all that already. It's just fallen off." Interestingly, this sense of declining influence was countered by several of the newer residents saying that there was more influence now than their used to be. Thus, rather than a steady decline in the residents' sense of influence, there have been ebbs and flows of declining and increasing influence.

Finances

The finances of the Association are rather complex and require some clarification. Prospective residents pay a one-time fee of $2,500 (that money can be borrowed from the association and paid back over time) and then pay monthly housing charges of 29 percent of their income for their units. These charges are recalculated every year to correspond to changes in residents' incomes. But this only amounts to a small portion of Mutual Housing's capitalization and finances. According to the NRC's model of Mutual Housing, the capital for development comes in the form of grants, usually from a state or city government. MHAs acquire and develop their properties with these grants without being burdened by long-term debt or mortgages. The model was realized in the development of Parkside Gables when

NHS received grants from the City of Stamford and the State Department of Housing to pay for the property's acquisition and development. Parkside Gables, therefore, was constructed as a debt-free development. This was the only time, however, that the model was fully implemented. In subsequent development projects, the Association has relied on a variety of funding sources, including loans, and their financing has resembled the patchwork of debt and leveraged capital of most CDC development work. There has been a substantial decline in the availability of public capital for affordable housing, both nationwide and in Connecticut. This public funding has been replaced, largely, by private, acquired through the Low-Income Housing Tax Credit program[7] and commercial loans.

The possibility of local control is greatly constrained by the lack of organizational fiscal self-sufficiency. That is, if organizations continuously need to go hat-in-hand to funding agencies—be they public, private, or not-for-profit—then the ability of the organizations to control their development and organizing projects will be constrained by those funders. Accordingly, fiscal self-sufficiency is a goal of all MHAs (and CLTs), but it has thus far been unrealized by those organizations. Mutual housing in Stamford seems unlikely to do so anytime soon.

Aside from residents' housing charges, the operating income of the Association can be broken down as follows: one-third corporate and foundation support; one-third to one-half development fees; one-third to one-sixth management fees. Two components of the Association's finances thus stand out: first, their inability to realize fiscal self-sufficiency, and their reliance on development fees as a primary source of capital; and second, their inability to fund developments with capital grants, instead using various forms of debt and tax credits. I will return to the implications of these later.

Who Lives in Mutual Housing in Stamford?

The residents of Parkside and Trinity are mixed in income and race, and they range from the very poor to the rather comfortably middle class. On balance, however, most are working, but with modest incomes, as the median annual household income of the residents is $24,273, and the mean is slightly higher at $27,187. While these income levels might seem rather high for affordable housing developments, the cost of living in Stamford is extremely high. Given the city's housing costs, the income needed for a market-rate one-bedroom rental unit to be affordable in Stamford is $45,400, and for a two-bedroom unit, that figure becomes $55,360 (National Low Income Housing Coalition, 2001). This means that the median household income in Mutual Housing is only 53.5 percent of the income needed to pay affordably for a one-bedroom unit in the Stamford metropolitan area, and only 43.8 percent for a two-bedroom. In this light, these

Table 4.2 Residents' Satisfaction with Mutual Housing

	Percent
Completely dissatisfied (1)	7.5
2	10
3	31.25
4	21.25
Completely satisfied (5)	30

incomes seem much more modest, and the need for affordable housing for these residents becomes clearer.

Residents' Satisfaction with Mutual Housing

One of the principal questions of this project is the simple one of, does mutual housing improve the lives of its residents? Based on the interviews with the residents, it is clear that the residents are generally satisfied with their housing situation (Table 4.2). And the results were similarly positive when the residents were asked to compare their current residency with their prior one (Table 4.3).

When the residents were asked the follow-up question of what they like the most about living in Mutual Housing, almost 40 percent of the residents stated that they liked the community involvement component of Mutual Housing more than anything else. A typical comment from a resident was, "I like the community and the tenant meetings. Any problems we have, we can solve among ourselves," or, "They always do things, meetings, and the annual celebration in the park. They care about the community; we have to do the cleaning." Interestingly, when the residents had been asked earlier why they decided to live in Mutual Housing, less than 20 percent said that community involvement was one of the reasons. So, to some extent there seems to be a transformative process at the level of the individual

Table 4.3 Comparing Current Residency with Prior One

	Percent
Significantly improved	50
Somewhat improved	22.5
About the same	11.25
Somewhat worsened	5
Significantly worsened	5
Don't know	6.25

residents, as they come to embrace notions of community through their participation in one. The comment that "we have to do the cleaning" also brings up the issue of home maintenance. Much of the literature on levels of satisfaction and housing tenure has highlighted the importance of home maintenance and repairs in building connections to one's dwelling and satisfaction in that dwelling (see, for instance, Galster, 1987; Saunders, 1990 and Rohe, McCarthy, and Van Vandt, 2000). But importantly, the work that mutual-housing residents do on home maintenance is at the level of the housing collective, rather than their own units. While this can help to build community among the residents, it can also serve to remind residents of their inability to make fundamental changes to the structure of their own particular units.

Along with the community involvement component of Mutual Housing, the residents were most satisfied with the 'dollars and cents' and 'bricks and mortar' aspects of their housing. That is, the units are affordable and satisfactory in quality, and this is a logical reflection of the centrality of people's interest in the quality of the amenities of their homes.

While the residents are generally satisfied with their units in mutual housing, when asked to do so, the residents also identified several problems. While many of those identified were site-specific (e.g. heating in Trinity), the two biggest criticisms might be lodged against the entire mutual housing model. The first was that it requires levels of resident participation that might not be realistically sustainable, and so residents stated, "It's supposed to be like you own your own home, but not everybody has that sense. Maybe the feeling of ownership they gave me, they're not giving it to some people moving in" or, "Well they want you on too many committees and I'm working." The second big problem is that the residents feel that the intensive interaction with the staff and other residents leaves them without enough of a sense of privacy and personal freedom. A typical comment was, "They want to know everything. They need your whole life story to live here," or, "There's no privacy. It's a lot of rules and regulations—probably too many, some justified, some not." These latter comments raise the related issue of the level of autonomy of the residents, which will be addressed shortly.

Resident Understandings of Mutual Housing and Traditional Forms of Housing Tenure

Questions remain, however, about whether these results could be found in other not-for-profit developed and managed housing. That is, is living in mutual housing substantially different from, and therefore an alternative to, traditional forms of housing tenure? Fully 80 percent of residents say they think it is. This, of course, begs the question of how it is different. In

Table 4.4 How Residents Think Mutual Housing
Is Different From Other Housing

	Percent
Community involvement/mission	46.6
Rules and regulations/no privacy	22.4
Affordability	15.5
Better apartment/building	8.6
Ownership security	3.5

response to this question (Table 4.4), residents essentially reiterated the concerns reported above. These ranged from those who identified (and supported) the community mission of the Association, to those who felt the rules and regulations governing the Association were too intrusive, so that it lacked the privacy that they would enjoy in most other forms of housing (except public housing, and some of the residents who had moved to mutual housing from public housing made exactly this argument—that mutual housing was too much like public housing).

The more explicit issue of housing tenure was also addressed, and the residents seem to have accepted the label of mutual housing as "enhanced rental" (Table 4.5) that sometimes comes from the staff. It is clear, however, that while the mutual housing is perceived by its residents as something different from the norm, it is not the tenureship that makes it different. When asked to explain their perceptions, most residents who identified as owners connected ownership with personal security (to stay and not be displaced). Most of the residents who felt like renters felt that way because of a lack of personal freedom over their daily housing decisions, like whether to paint the walls a different color.

The Potential and Limits of Collective Ownership of Housing

Several basic conclusions emerge out of this chapter, and while some of these will be discussed in the concluding chapter, they need to be introduced here.

Table 4.5 Residents' Perception of Their Housing Tenure

	Percent
Owner	23.75
Renter	60
Neither	16.25

First, the collective ownership of housing is economically and politically viable. There has been substantial growth in the last fifteen years in the number of organizations that are taking direct ownership over housing. This growth in organizations, and the cases presented here, demonstrate that these organizations are viable forms of affordable housing production. Given that the for-profit real-estate market is unable to produce enough adequate, affordable housing, MHAs, CLTs and limited-equity co-ops are among the most fiscally frugal ways in which it can be constructed and maintained. There are three reasons for this. First, if the property and units can be acquired or developed using capital grants, then the housing is free of long-term debt servicing and can be maintained much more cheaply. Second, even if the housing needs to be acquired using loans and investments instead of grants, collective ownership means that the units will not revert back to market prices when residents move out or time-limited affordability requirements expire. Thus, the initial subsidies involved in producing the unit, in whatever form they take, are never lost.

Third, many forms of affordable housing provision—particularly those that are geared toward homeownership—don't have a structure in place that insures the long-term maintenance of the housing units. Problems arise when low-income homeowners are faced with large-scale repairs and unexpected costs they cannot afford (and it should be noted that some small-scale limited-equity co-operatives have run into the same problems of lack of capital for large repairs—see Matloff, 2002). The result is often either a poorly maintained or distressed property, or the displacement of the resident because of an inability to pay the repairs and the other costs of homeownership (for a useful discussion of this, see Meyer, Yeager, and Burayidi, 1994). In contrast, these collectives are frameworks that can protect the long-term maintenance of the units, as well as their long-term affordability.

So if collectives are viable, then the next questions become: Does collective ownership allow the residents to realize local autonomy and does this framework promote the process of equitable development? The answers to these questions that emerge from the cases are more ambiguous than the answers to the first one, and require a good deal more discussion.

Collective ownership does promote a greater degree of local control. That is, it provides a shelter from the flows of investment and disinvestment that can be so detrimental to the housing options available to low-income people. The cases discussed here all emerged in the contradictory context prevalent in many cities of prohibitively expensive housing costs coexisting with long-term and systemic disinvestment in the affordable housing stock. In the MHASWC, Parkside Gables was developed in place of a hodgepodge of abandoned or nearly abandoned houses. Trinity Park was renovated after it was condemned due to almost thirty years' lack of maintenance and repairs by its owner. These developments, and the units within them, are now largely immune from the processes of housing inflation and housing disinvestment.

The possibility of local autonomy, however, extends beyond simply the ability of local-scale actors to mitigate the effects of capital flows or to create shelters from those flows. The establishment and growth of mutual housing in Stamford and the CLT in Burlington have partially *transformed* the West Side and the Old North End as places. The stability of the housing, in terms of both their insulation from capital flows and the length of residency of the members, has helped change the identity of the areas. When the mutual housing residents were asked if they thought mutual housing was active in the West Side, many responded, "We *are* the West Side." And the role of Mutual Housing residents and organizers in working on the Mill River development plan, the neighborhood watch, the creation of the community garden, and the rehabbing of the community pool in the Yerwood Center and of Carwin Park cannot be overestimated. At the same time, it is unclear whether this role in place-making was a result of the form of ownership of the housing, or the result of rather traditional organizing efforts that could have been undertaken by any CDC, regardless of how they structure the tenure of their housing. What is clear, however, is that while most CDCs are increasingly less interested in organizing and the concept of community control, organizing and resident/community control are structured into these collectives in ways that do not exist in traditional CDCs.

That does not mean, however, that resident organizing efforts remain constant if attention is focused elsewhere. This mutual housing case provides ample evidence for the truism that organizing efforts need to be constantly sustained if they are to continue to exist, let alone flourish. But the time and efforts needed to organize detracts from the ability of collectives to focus on the goals of new development (and this is one of the ways in CLTs and MHAs differ from co-ops, that is, expansion is an inherent goal of the former and not of the latter). When combined with the fact that these groups depend on their development fees for their financial viability, this becomes a central contradiction in their work and one of the most significant barriers to local autonomy. That is, on the one hand, local autonomy requires the mobilization of the residents and the other people and institutions that constitute "the local." But on the other hand, fiscal self-sufficiency requires new development and the income associated with that development, which means that less time and labor can go toward the organizing needed for such mobilization.

The financing of the collectives also raises real questions for the possibility of local autonomy. While the models of collective ownership are fiscally frugal, they are still forms of affordable housing construction. As such, they need to be subsidized, as do all forms of adequate affordable housing. This reality, however, inherently places them in positions of financial dependence, which certainly limit the potential for local control. At the same time, if these organizations are consistently looking to develop new properties in order to generate revenues, then this also means that the decisions being made within these organizations are responding to the interests of profitability, rather than collective control and political empowerment. This is most evident by the relatively inverse relationship between new development activities and commitment to organizing.

Further barriers to local autonomy are apparent in this chapter. First, the level of control and influence of the residents in mutual housing is clearly less than what the organizations' structure might indicate. This limits the diversity of the perspectives included in the production of the local. Second, while the collectives might insulate their housing from the vagaries of the market, they cannot do so for other properties that exist locally. And one of the problems faced by both mutual housing in Stamford and the CLT in Burlington has been finding affordable new sites to develop. Increasing property costs in both contexts—which to some extent reflect their success in improving conditions in the neighborhoods where they have worked—have made that task much more difficult. As Mary Houghton, finance director of the Burlington CLT has stated, "We can stabilize housing prices for our residents, but the larger market is skyrocketing; it's in a cycle we can't begin to keep up with" (PolicyLink, 2002).

Third, the meanings of the housing, property, and ownership in the collectives are still largely the dominant, hegemonic constructions (the properties might be taken off the market, but never fully—and they are all, in the first instance, purchased) and so the ultimate form of autonomy, the ability to create a set of meanings at odds with the hegemonic ones, is not yet realized. This is why one of the Lower East Side squats refused to go co-op, and one resident in one of the new co-ops has decided not to participate and will continue his residency as a tenant, not resident-owner. Theoretically this could be overcome by the proliferation of the collective-ownership model. But the reproduction of this model will not challenge dominant sets of meanings if those involved do not understand what they are doing as counterhegemonic. Most of these collectives work very hard to "mainstream" themselves—often for funding purposes (this point is made rather forcefully by Krinsky and Hovde, 1996). Also, while a significant number of mutual housing residents saw themselves as living in a completely different form of housing, over 80 percent viewed themselves in terms of the usual housing tenure framework. This issue also begs the important question of whether needed state support would ever continue if the model itself challenged any hegemonic constructions of property. In all of the cases discussed here, the extent of state support for their efforts played a key role in their abilities to realize their goals—particularly in Burlington and New York (even if in New York that state role changed dramatically over time). But if these collectives were to grow enough to challenge the dominant frameworks of property, then that success might undercut the state support which is often such a big part of making it possible.

The potential for housing collectives to realize local autonomy is therefore somewhat mixed—although it is perhaps greater than in the other forms of collectives discussed in this book. To some extent the collectives and organizing that go with them have altered the shape and meanings of their localities. But their abilities to control the larger flows of capital in their local real-estate market, or their political potential to transform the meaning of housing and property, have been more limited. They have unquestionably, however, improved the lives of the residents who live within them—and have given those residents a degree of control over their lives that would not be possible otherwise. These are perhaps the most powerful arguments in support of collective housing, and ones that should not be downplayed or dismissed.

CHAPTER 5

Collective Ownership of Money

We survived, and when everybody else was leaving,
we stayed. That's what I'm most proud of.
—Elly Spangenberg, Bethex FCU board president

As a response to the failure of private financial institutions to equitably meet the needs of large segments of the American population, alternative financial institutions have been created to meet those needs by using different sets of logics and organizing principles. The largest group of these organizations, loosely referred to as Community Development Financial Institutions (CDFIs), have mostly been created with the goal of bringing investment capital to low-income areas that have struggled with capital flight, redlining, and long-term disinvestment. A second set are local currencies, often called Local Exchange Trading Systems (LETS), and are alternative currencies based on place-bound economic relations and mutual trust. This chapter begins by analyzing how the economic restructuring of the last quarter century has dramatically increased the separation between people at the local level and financial institutions, and left low-income people and communities without retail financial services. It then briefly discusses LETS in general and presents the case of Ithaca Hours, which is a LETS system in Ithaca, New York. It then describes the different types of CDFIs and their attributes. The chapter then focuses on one type of CDFI: the community development credit union (CDCU) and its history, structure, and impact in the United States. From there, it presents a case study of one CDCU, Bethex Federal Credit Union in the South Bronx, and concludes by assessing the potential and limits of the collective ownership of money to allow low-income people to realize local autonomy and economic justice.

The Restructuring of Financial Institutions
and the Lack of Services in Low-Income Areas

The economic crises of the 1970s were manifest in particular ways with regards to the financial services sector. The growth of inflation and the collapse of Bretton Woods[1] in the early 1970s meant that the interest rates paid for large depositors in banks were now no longer acceptable from the point of view of the investor. The interest rates paid by banks at this time were capped by government regulation, and as interest rates grew through the 1970s and into the 1980s, the gap between what banks could legally pay investors and what investors could find elsewhere became more substantial (Avery, 1991). Consequently, individuals with significant sums of capital began to invest directly in financial markets, facilitated by the emergence of savings vehicles like money market mutual funds. The growth in corporate bonds in the 1970s also meant that large borrowers were no longer dependent on banks for access to capital, as they were able to bypass the "middleman" of banks and go directly to the investors.

In the 1970s, banks face increased competition for both their sources of capital and profit, and this meant that banks needed to restructure in order to stay competitive. Since their ability to compete based on return on investments was limited, a principal component of restructuring was the rapid growth in the number of bank branches so as to offer more convenience and services to attract depositors. In the aggregate, in the period from 1975 to 1985, the total number of bank offices nationwide grew an astonishing 38 percent (Avery, Bostic, Calem, and Canner, 1997). But this growth was extremely unevenly distributed, as high-income areas experienced a growth of over 60 percent, whereas low-income ones witnessed less than 8 percent growth (Figure 5.1).

Things began to change in the mid-1980s and, as a result of several processes, the 1980s and 1990s saw an end to the growth in branches. First, there was a flurry of financial institution mergers and acquisitions. Second, the late 1980s was a period of substantial failure, bankruptcy, and closure of financial institutions (especially savings and loan associations). Third, deregulation brought down the legal firewalls that had existed between banks and nonbank financial institutions as well as those that had limited the size of suprastate banks. So while the period from 1975 to 1985 was one of very rapid growth in the number of retail banking offices nationwide, the period from 1985 to 1995 saw a modest contraction in those numbers. In the aggregate, the total number of offices nationwide fell over 6 percent, but again, this was very unevenly distributed (Figure 5.2), as the number in high-income areas actually *rose* almost 6 percent, while those in low-income areas plummeted by over 25 percent (Avery, Bostic, Calem, and Canner, 1997). Overall, the result was that, "Increased options for bor-

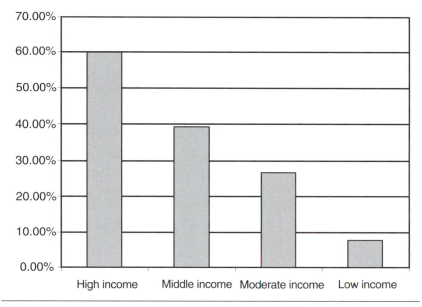

Figure 5.1 Change in the Distribution of Bank Offices, 1975–1985 (by zip code income[2])
Source: Avery, Bostic, Calem, and Canner, 1997

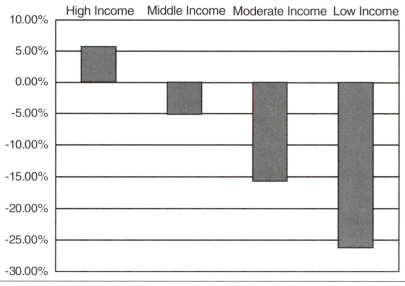

Figure 5.2 Changes in the Distribution of Bank Branches, 1985–1995 (by zip code income)
Source: Avery, Bostic, Calem, and Canner, 1997

rowing and saving benefited large sophisticated savers and borrowers. Smaller savers and borrowers involved diseconomies of scale for banks" (Dymski and Veitch, 1996, p. 1246).

Finally, it would clearly be inadequate to discuss the distribution of commercial financial services in American cities and not address the issue of race. Aside from the industry's restructuring, what makes the 1970s particularly important in the history of banking, are the substantial political and legal victories realized by those who organized and struggled against the practice of financial institution redlining and racial discrimination. Redlining refers to the practice of commercial banks in which they would systematically deny mortgage credit to any person within certain areas—almost invariably nonwhite areas—regardless of their individual credit worthiness.[3] The efforts of these organizers yielded the 1975 passage of the Federal Home Mortgage Loan Disclosure Act and the 1977 Community Reinvestment Act (CRA) (Squires, 1992), and these acts required that banks keep records of their loan decisions and invest capital back into the places where they obtain capital in the form of deposits, respectively. In the years since 1977, community organizations have been able to use the CRA to extract more than $350 billion in agreements with financial institutions to get capital into low-income neighborhoods where it otherwise would not go (Immergluck, 1999; Schwartz, 1998; Shlay, 1999). But despite the successes of the CRA, mortgage lending remains a very racialized process, and, according to the banks' own data, blacks are still 60 percent more likely to be denied a mortgage loan than whites—all else being equal (Browne and Tootell, 1995; Munnell, Tootell, Browne and McEneaney, 1996).

But CRA and antiredlining struggles tend to focus on access to loans—particularly home mortgage loans. While the structured absence of mortgage capital can unquestionably devastate a neighborhood, given that the median *total* net-worth[4]—the difference between families' gross assets and their liabilities—of non-home-owning families in the United States is only $4,200 (Kennickell, Starr-McCluer, and Surette, 2000), it is clear that most inner-city renters are not in positions to buy a home. Their needs as consumers of financial services are much more modest than a mortgage loan and include building some personal savings, having a checking account, and borrowing small sums of money for emergencies and vacations. The diminishing number of branches in low-income areas certainly constrain their ability to meet those consumer needs.

Probably just as important as the declining number of bank offices, however, are the increasing barriers (in the form of bank fee structures and minimum balance requirements) that have accompanied financial institution restructuring over the past twenty years. These obstacles, largely invisible to wealthier savers and investors, have effectively prohibited many low-income people from access to those institutions. Nationwide, 25 percent of low-income families do not have any kind of transaction (checking or savings) account with a financial institution, and that over 55 percent (of low-income families) do not have a credit card (Hogarth and O'Donnell, 1999). Unsurprisingly, among the poorest of the poor, the statistics worsen, and about 40 percent of families with incomes of less than $10,000 a year do not have a checking account (Doyle, Lopez and Saidenberg, 1998).

A major component of the changes in retail banking that have left low-income communities underserved has been a dramatic increase in the size of financial institutions and a loss of smaller to mid-sized banks. From the mid-1970s to the mid-1990s, the number of banks in the country plunged from 18,600 to 12,200. Most of this decline was among small, single-office—that is, local—banks. Over this period, the percent of all banks that are single-office banks plummeted from 58 percent to 40 percent, and single-office banks now account for less than 6 percent of all bank offices (Avery, Bostic, Calen, and Canner, 1997). The Financial Modernization Act of 1999 brought significant changes to the structure of American banking, and tore down the remaining firewalls that had separated banks from other nonbank financial institutions like insurance companies, securities firms, and trust companies (consequently weakening the CRA, which does not apply to nonbank financial institutions). It therefore has furthered the process of consolidation and growth of America's largest financial institutions. The size of America's largest financial institutions have thus swelled dramatically to become far and away the largest in the world. Whereas in 1990, only 2 of the 15 world's largest financial institutions were American, by 2001, the overwhelming majority were (*The Economist*, 2002). And this growth has largely been the result of mergers and acquisitions due to deregulation through the 1980s and 1990s—culminating in the Financial Modernization Act in 1999.

In this context, increasingly larger, multipurpose—often multinational—financial institutions are disconnected from any locality and often exclude poor and nonwhite communities, so that alternatives have emerged. These alternative, and collective, forms of finance have taken two very different forms. First, have been Local Exchange Trading Systems (LETS), and second are Community Development Financial Institutions (CDFI)—and Community Development Credit Unions (CDCUs) in particular. The latter group, however, have been much more significant and widespread—particularly in low-income communities—and thus make up the bulk of this chapter.

Local Currencies

There is a long history of people using localized scrips (forms of currencies) in times and places of systemic economic crises—most notably in

American history during the Great Depression, but striking recent examples from around the world are their emergence in Argentina since that country fell into crisis in 2001 and Russia after the collapse of the Soviet Union. These localized currencies are structured, usually cooperatively and not-for-profit, forms of exchange, in which people who are time-rich and cash-poor can be socially and economically productive despite their lack of nationally backed money. As Offe and Heinze (1992, p. 95) describe such a system:

> It offers both the unemployed and everybody else the opportunity of transforming their labor power or working time into purchasing power *without* the necessity of either working for an employing firm or of possessing capital, which is a *sine quo non* of earning a living by self-employment.

The contemporary American forms that such localized currencies take can broadly be referred to as Local Exchange Trading Systems (LETS), Time Dollars, or the Ithaca Hours model. While there are (often significant) differences between them, for our purposes here, I will discuss them together and refer to them as LETS. LETS were created in the early 1980s in Vancouver Island, British Columbia, in Canada in a town that was suffering from the relocation and closure of its two main sources of employment (a timber mill and U.S. Air Force base). LETS are forms of self-contained networks in which members buy or sell services to other members and are paid in the LETS currency. In most LETS, every member has an individual account, which records their debt or credit. Members do not "owe" the person or business providing the service, instead their debt is to the LETS system, and their debt is therefore socialized. Also, LETS do not yield any form of interest, and so there is no incentive to accumulate LETS credits. In most LETS, the debts and credits of the individual members are published regularly, and the regulation of the membership—to make sure that there is no "free rider" problem—is done through the combination of mutual trust and codependence, and peer pressure. For all of these reasons, LETS are inherently local systems. That is precisely the point—to trade and consume locally, and many have specific geographic boundaries to their use. Local currencies are often very explicitly touted as a "response to the globalization of capitalism" (Pacione, 1997), and it has been argued that "the principal economic objective of a LETS is to facilitate 'import substitution' in its locality in order to promote a local economy that is less reliant on external sources of goods, service and money" (Pacione, 1999, p. 68). LETS currencies are meant to thus be used simultaneously with the national currency, and transactions often take place with both currencies—with the component of the service that is local being paid for in LETS and that which is extralocal paid for in dollars (in the U.S.). For instance, a plumber provides the service of replacing a person's kitchen sink pipes. In a LETS framework, the time of the service provider is paid for in the local currency, while the parts needed for the job are paid for in the national currency.

In the last twenty years, local currencies have grown dramatically in size and number, and there are now about 1,900 local currencies operating around the world, including over 100 in the United States (Lietaer, 2001). Perhaps the largest and most influential of these is Ithaca Hours in the Finger Lakes of upstate New York—which claims to have over 60 local currencies modeled after it.

Ithaca Hours

Ithaca, New York, is a small town on the southern tip of Cayuga Lake in the Finger Lakes. Like Burlington, Vermont (discussed in chapter 4), it is a famously politically progressive town, which combines a significant university presence with the very real, and visible, problems of urban poverty and underemployment. Ithaca has been called "America's Most Enlightened Town" by the *Utne Reader* (Spayde, 1997), and elected an openly socialist mayor through the early 1990s. It is also a town with an incredible density of alternative forms of living and working, which includes a land trust, had been a home for many countercultural communes in the late 1960s (discussed in chapter 2), several forms of consumer cooperatives, several CDCUs, and an EcoVillage—a housing cooperative combined with organic farming and other "green" activities.

In this context, during the recession of 1991, Paul Glover, a local resident and activist, founded Ithaca Hours. Ithaca Hours are real printed currency, unlike many other LETS and Time Dollars, where the transactions—and their debts and credits—are inscribed into ledgers. Each Ithaca Hour note is the equivalent of $10, which is the average hourly wage in Tomkins County (where Ithaca is located). The currency comes in multiple fractions of the Hour, to facilitate transactions. Each transaction is negotiated by the two parties, so some professional services cost more than one Hour for one hour's work. Every new member receives one new Ithaca Hour—or two, if they agree to be listed in the directory of participating businesses and service providers—and every eight months, members can apply for an additional hour to reward their participation. In this way, the money supply grows, but in a controlled manner. Businesses and individuals who receive Hours as part of their income have to report it as such to the IRS. Finally, Hours are distinctly spatially defined and they can only be used within an area in a 20-mile radius from Ithaca's city center.

In the years since its creation, Ithaca Hours has grown dramatically—often as a result of working with, and through, other local organizations. For instance, Alternatives Federal Credit Union (a local CDCU) provided

Mr. Glover with a VISTA position from 1993 to 1995, which played an important role early in the organization's history by allowing him to work on Ithaca Hours while receiving a paycheck. Alternatives also absorbed the currency's operating expenses at the time. Also, the city's Chamber of Commerce accepts payment for services in Hours. In 1998, the advisory board of Ithaca Hours incorporated into a not-for-profit corporation, which has furthered both Ithaca Hours' growth, and its links to other organizations in the community. The corporation has the ability to make grants up to 11 percent of the Hours in circulation to local groups or organizations. Thus far, twenty-two different organizations have received grants in the form of Hours from the corporation. In 1999, Ithaca Hours spun off a member-owned "Ithaca Health Fund," a form of localized health insurance—and whose members receive discounts from many of the city's health-care providers. Finally, Alternatives received the largest loan ever in a local currency in 2000, when it borrowed 3,000 Hours to help finance its new headquarters in the city. Ithaca Hours now has over 400 participating businesses, 1,500 individuals, and 9,000 Hours ($90,000) in circulation. This is, admittedly, relatively small in scale when you consider that Ithaca has 30,000 people who have an annual aggregate income of over $388 million. This is an issue we will return to later.

Community Development Financial Institutions

The second set of alternatives to emerge to fill the gaps left by mainstream financial institutions are community development financial institutions (CDFIs). These institutions have been created to redirect capital back into low-income areas that have suffered from capital flight and structural disinvestment by traditional banks. Generally speaking, there are five principal types of CDFIs currently operating in the United States: Community Development Banks; Community Development Credit Unions; Community Development Loan Funds; Microenterprise Loan Funds; and Community Development Venture Capital funds. These different types of CDFIs perform different kinds of functions, and range in size from small, volunteer-run, and church-based CDCUs to the much larger community-development banks—such as the Los Angeles Community Development Bank, which was created with $435 million from the federal government (Sass Rubin and Stankiewicz, 2000). While this is not the place for a summary of the different CDFIs, their history, and how they operate (see Gunn and Gunn, 1991; Parzen and Kieschnick, 1992; Tholin, 1994, for useful discussions of this), a few key points must be made about CDFIs. First, they have grown rapidly and dramatically over the last fifteen years. A survey of their membership by the National Community Capital Association found that their assets had grown roughly twentyfold from 1989 to 1999 (National Community Capital Association, 1999). This growth has continued, and from 1999 to 2001, their assets grew by an additional 41 percent (Hawke, 2002). The growth of CDFIs has been driven, in part, by public sector support for this sector. Second, they all play an intermediary role between outside investors and borrowers in low-income communities. They therefore act to pool "outside" capital, and invest it into communities where it largely would not go otherwise. Third, of these five different CDFIs, only two (community development banks and CDCUs) actually provide retail banking services and act as depository institutions. The remaining three instead act solely as investment vehicles. But community-development banks, while more willing to invest in low-income areas than most banks, are still banks, and they act accordingly—and require a bank's startup capital. CDCUs, conversely, are collectively owned not-for-profit corporations, which have the added benefit of requiring almost no startup capital. Of all the types of CDFIs, they are the ones most likely to allow low-income people to act collectively to realize greater control over their financial lives. CDCUs, while performing many of the same functions as banks, do so with very different logic, since not only are they not profit-motivated, but they also have an explicit community development focus.

Community Development Credit Unions

History

Community-development credit unions are a component of the credit-union industry, but are distinguished from the majority of this industry both in the composition of their memberships and their locations. Credit unions have a relatively long history in the United States, and the first credit union was formed in 1908 (Williams, 1997). Their creation was influenced both by the emergence of the institutions in Canada, and the proliferation of mutual aid societies that had been constructed in many immigrant communities in the United States.[5] The earliest, and oldest (some are still in existence) community development credit unions were created in segregated black areas in the rural south during the Great Depression, many of these organized in churches. The number of credit unions grew dramatically in the 1960s as the Office of Economic Opportunity (OEO) created around 400 between 1964 and 1973 (Robinson and Gilson, 1993). As a reflection of that growth, CDCUs formed their own trade association in 1974, the National Federation of Community Development Credit Unions (NFCDCU). While most of the OEO-created credit unions failed during the 1970s and 1980s, the CDCU movement was continuously being reborn, first by groups organizing around redlining issues in the 1970s and then, in the 1980s, as responses to the withdrawal of federal support from low-income cities and neighborhoods, and the closing of bank branches that was part of the restructuring of, and mergers between, financial institutions (Rosenthal, 1994).

The last decade has been a period of substantial growth for CDCUs. They benefited from increased public support both from the National Credit Union Administration (which is the federal agency responsible for regulating and insuring credit unions), as it established the Office of Community Development Credit Unions in 1993, and from the 1994 creation of the National CDFI fund. The number of Low-Income Credit Unions (LICUs)[6] grew from 244 in 1990 to 356 in 1996 and was up to 912 in 2002 (Williams, 1998, NCUA, n.d.). The growth in the number of LICUs has been mirrored by the growth of their total assets, which grew through the 1990s and *tripled* from 1999 to 2001 (Hawke, 2002).

Structure

CDCUs are member-owned and, theoretically at least, controlled not-for-profit financial institutions. Like other credit unions, they are federally or state chartered, regulated, and insured. CDCUs serve two primary purposes: to provide financial services, like access to savings and checking accounts, to areas underserved by traditional commercial financial institutions; and to provide loans that promote community development in the places in which their members are located.

CDCUs tend to be small-scale institutions, some with less than $1,000,000 in total assets, and 64 percent of them possessing total assets of less than five million dollars (Tansey, 2001). But CDCUs can range in size to over $40,000,000, the size of the Self-Help Credit Union in North Carolina (National Federation of Community Development Credit Unions, 1999). CDCUs get their capital from three sources: members' deposits (both individual and organizational members), capital grants (used as equity to startup or expand and can come from the state, commercial financial institutions, or foundations), and nonmember deposits (which come primarily from foundations and commercial financial institutions). This ability to accept nonmember deposits makes them different from most other credit unions, which cannot accept such moneys. While most CDCUs obtain the majority of their capital from individual members' deposits, nonmember deposits are essential to the growth, and often the survival of, CDCUs, and this is especially true of very small institutions (those with less than $500,000 in assets). Despite the important role played by nonmember deposits, Low-Income Credit Unions receive only between 5 and 13 percent of their assets from nonmember deposits, with smaller CDCUs receiving a greater share of their assets from this source than larger ones (Williams, 1998).

While credit unions need little startup or overhead capital, there are higher costs associated with serving low-income communities (smaller accounts, more frequent transactions, smaller loans, financial advising, etc.), than more affluent ones. The ability of the smaller CDCUs to survive despite their limited assets and higher transaction costs often comes from the role of sponsoring organizations (often churches) in absorbing operating costs (like providing a staff) and providing reserves to cover losses realized from bad loans. However, many sponsoring organizations don't have the capital to cover these costs, and so they rely on member volunteers to staff the credit unions. While this can be a powerful vehicle for building a sense of community, it can also limit the potential of the credit unions to provide enough loans and services to attract more members. The cycle can be a difficult one to break. Assets are needed to employ a staff to provide services, but assets can be accumulated only if there is a staff in place to attract enough members and their deposits. Outside infusions of capital in either grant or nonmember deposit forms often provide the means to break out of the cycle.

Like all other credit unions, CDCUs can make loans only to their members. These loans tend to be small in size and geared toward the consumer needs of the membership, although CDCUs do some lending for business and microenterprise development. The amount of business lending is fairly limited, however, due to both the costs and risks associated with small-business lending, and to legal constraints on CDCUs that limit their abilities to lend to "nonnatural people," that is, corporations of any kind (Berkowitz, 1997). Because of the small size of most credit unions, their loan portfolios, and their individual loans, it is extremely difficult to estimate the aggregate economic impact of the lending activity of CDCUs in the United States. We do know a few things about the loan portfolios of CDCUs. The average loan portfolio size for LICUs in 1998 was about $4.5 million, but the median was much smaller, only $785,000 (Williams, 1998). Somewhat smaller numbers were reported by the NFCDCU, which claims that its membership has an average loan portfolio of about $1.5 million (National Federation of Community Development Credit Unions, n.d.). The delinquency rates of CDCU loans hover under two percent, with charge-off rates of .8 percent—which does not compare too unfavorably with the .6 percent reported by the FDIC for all its insured banks nationwide (Tansey, 2001).

Most traditional credit unions define "fields of membership" (FOM) that provide access to membership only to people who are within this defined field (usually a workplace, or common union membership, etc.). CDCUs, and LICUs, are able to define FOMs that are more loosely structured, as long as more than half of their members earn less than 80 percent of the area's median income. CDCU membership is thus much more open than at most credit unions, and this is done without threatening the tax-exempt status of the CDCUs. These members, as low-income people, very often lack access to any other financial institution.

Governance and decision-making in CDCUs are organized in a fairly straightforward manner. The credit unions' members own the credit union by virtue of their membership. Like most co-ops, control is structured in a one-person, one-vote formula, and someone's ability to influence credit-union policy is not determined by the size of their account. The credit union is governed by a board of directors, elected by the membership according to the CDCU's bylaws. A supervisory committee and a credit committee oversee the credit union's operations, insuring that the bylaws and all state and federal laws are being followed, and observing lending decisions, respectively. There may or may not be an employed staff that handles daily operations.

So the credit-union model has a fairly lengthy set of experiences, demonstrating that despite severe limitations, it is a viable framework that has been adopted and used in hundreds of places throughout the United States. But their ability to survive and grow does not necessarily mean that they have empowered people in the places in which they are located or even improved the lives of those people. To address these issues, a case study of the Bethex Federal Credit Union in the South Bronx will make up the bulk of the remainder of this chapter.

Bethex Federal Credit Union

The South Bronx

The story of the South Bronx is familiar to many people. Much of the area was literally burned-out during the 1970s. The suburban exodus of whites that was such a dominant feature of the American urban landscape in the 1960s and 1970s was more conspicuous here than in perhaps any other neighborhood or city in the country. The total population of the six Community Boards that make up the South Bronx fell from 764,400 in the 1970 Census to 453,796 in 1980—a plummet of more than 40 percent in a mere ten years. In sections such as Hunt's Point and Morrisiana, it fell by more than 60 percent. The decline in population was matched by the unprecedented destruction of the housing stock, as much of the area was burned down by arsonists—often working for landlords who felt they could get the best return on their investment by collecting the insurance money a fire would bring. This is the story of the South Bronx that has been so vividly etched into the consciousness of the American public, by President Carter's visit in 1977, by Reagan's use of the government's failure to improve the area as part of his 1980 campaign, by movies like *Fort Apache: The Bronx* and books like *Bonfire of the Vanities*.

But the story continues, and by the late 1980s and early 1990s, the South Bronx had begun a process of redevelopment, as houses started going up in large numbers and commercial activities began to reappear (Grogan and Proscio, 2000; Hall, 1999; Horowitz, 1994; José Vergara, 1989; Mittelbach, 1993; McKee, 1995; *Planning*, 1996). In the period from the late 1980s to 1998, 57,000 new units of affordable housing were built or rehabbed in the Bronx—with the vast majority of this construction occurring in the South Bronx (Ferrer, 1998). The economic recovery of the South Bronx was driven largely by a set of public investments in housing—primarily in partnerships between the city government and the dense network of CDCs that had emerged in the 1970s and 1980s (and even earlier). And while there are still the basic problems of persistently high unemployment, poverty among those who work, a continued shortage of affordable housing, and massive environmental and health concerns, the South Bronx is certainly not burning anymore. Just as the death of the Bronx in the 1970s was made nationally visible by the visits of Carter and Reagan, its rebirth in the 1990s was marked by visits by President Clinton in both 1997 and 1999. Therefore just as the South Bronx was the national poster child for "urban decay" in the 1970s and early 1980s, so too has it become the celebrated icon of "the [capitalist] revolution of the damned," community self-help, and community bootstrapism.

Finally, despite the economic recovery that the Bronx has realized in the last ten years, financial institutions have continued to relate to it, at best, at arms-length. Substantial parts of the borough do not contain a single bank branch, and the South Bronx has about one-eighth the density of bank branches per person as the nationwide average. It is in this context, of a place dying and reborn (with substantial public support but little attention from banks), that Bethex both emerged and now has flourished.

History

The Bethex Federal Credit Union was founded in 1970 by several women on welfare associated with both the Bethany Church[7] and a Board of Education–sponsored school for welfare recipients. The initial goals of the credit union were fairly small-scale, focused on allowing the women on welfare to establish small savings accounts and borrow money for emergencies. The credit union went through a very difficult period in the 1970s and 1980s. The church, which formally sponsored the credit union, asked it to leave under the pretense that the credit union's members were not joining the congregation. It has always been suspected within the credit union, however, that the reason for the ejection was that the church was a Caribbean black congregation, and the credit union's membership consisted (at that point) almost entirely of American blacks. After its ejection, the credit union successively occupied many different homes, including (among other places) Joy Cousminer's apartment (one of the founders and its current manager and treasurer), a Medicaid clinic's basement, a burned-out building on Willis Avenue, another church, and the basement of a Manufacturers Hanover bank. This mobility was such a dominant feature of those years that Bethex was jokingly referred to by one former board member as, "a gypsy credit union." The credit union's existence was thus extremely precarious in this period, and the context of the credit union struggling to survive in the midst of the abandonment of the South Bronx in the 1970s needs to be reasserted. But the credit union continued operating and never closed it doors (even when it didn't have any).

Conditions at the credit union began to improve in the late 1980s and early 1990s. The organization moved into its current location, in the basement of a housing development of the Mount Hope CDC, 1993. The CU's membership began to grow steadily at this point, as it was able to realize an operational stability that had not been possible before, and Bethex is currently fairly large by CDCU standards.

Along with this now-fixed location, Bethex's growth in the 1990s was driven by relationships that the credit union began to establish with a variety of other institutions, both locally and extralocally. Cooperative Home Care Associates, the worker-owned company described in chapter 3, established a relationship with Bethex that made membership in the credit union attractive to its worker-owners. Also, when the Northwest Bronx Community and Clergy Coalition's credit union failed in 1993, Bethex was offered their members by the NCUA. Bethex has also come to act as the credit union for several other small churches, which do not have the population or the capacity to establish their own CDCUs. Bethex is thus a bit unusual for a CDCU in that it has a multiple group FOM that extends beyond its immediately local area. The credit union has also established relationships with several public elementary schools in the area, allowing their students to begin savings accounts, and, perhaps most importantly, teaching them how to manage their money and how to interact with a financial institution. This program alone has generated around 1,500 student-members of the credit union, as well as enhanced the visibility of the credit union in the Bronx. Finally, in a unique partnership, Bethex has established a relationship with two check-cashing chains to allow its members to conduct transactions at eight check-cashing stores around the south Bronx—instead of having their members come to one of the branches of the credit union. Thus, while the initial place-based linkage with Bethany church was lost, Bethex has replaced this with several other localized relationships and ties. And in this sense, Bethex is a cluster of localized communities rather than *a community*.

These connections aside, the most important relationships that Bethex has been able to establish have been with the state. This began in 1989 with a grant of $100,000 from New York State, earmarked to do business loans. This was followed up by a few small annual grants from the state used for loan-loss, operating costs, and, in the last few years, an Individual Development Account (IDA) program. The larger grants, however, have come from Washington, not Albany, and since the creation of the federal CDFI Fund, Bethex has received two grants from this fund. The first was awarded in 1996 for $100,000. In 1998 Bethex received the second grant of $460,000 for the explicit goal of opening a branch in Mott Haven. That branch has opened, as have two other branches in the South Bronx and one in upper Manhattan.

All of this has meant that Bethex's membership has grown dramatically in the last decade. There are currently about 10,000 members of the credit union (if you include the schoolchildren), and approximately 100 new members join the credit union each month. This growth has both been facilitated by, and constitutive of, an increasing professionalization of the board and staff of the credit union. But this has also raised substantial issues about the governance of the credit union.

Governance

As in most corporations, there are distinctions between the role of the board and the role of the staff in the running of the credit union. But this has not always been the case. Until the 1990s, there was no staff at Bethex, and all the operational work was done by the board and by other member-volunteers. Through the course of the last decade, a staff has grown steadily. With the growth in the staff has come a transformation of the board of directors, which has changed from an operational board to a board that is concerned with longer-term sets of issues and problems, and which has the ability to leave day-to-day operations to the staff and manager. This transformation, however, has affected not only the roles the board needs to play but also the composition of the board members. The board has become divided between the long-term members and newer community-development professionals. The two board members who mediate this division are the current board president, Elly Spangenberg, and the credit union manager and board treasurer, Joy Cousminer. Both are founding members of the credit union, as well as being well educated, so they therefore seem to have legitimacy in both camps on the board. In practice the board is controlled not by the credit union's members, but by its staff (as embodied in Ms. Cousminer) and the professional developers who have relatively recently joined it.

The failure of the credit union's members to control the board is a reflection of the overall lack of member control of the credit union. Despite their technical ownership and the authority that is structurally supposed to correspond with that ownership, the members of the Bethex credit union appear to exhibit relatively little control over the institution. Theoretically, the board is elected by will of the membership at the annual meetings. The annual meetings, however, are much more social than democratic gatherings. The election process is largely a formality, as anyone who is interested in becoming involved in the credit union's governance is able to do so. At the same time, however, nominations to the board are not accepted from the floor at the meeting. Board membership is also not open to any member. Instead it is required that anyone interested in becoming a board member must first serve on a committee for some, unspecified, period of time. The board members whose three-year terms were up at the annual meeting I attended were reelected without debate or formal discussion. The members who attended did not do so to control the credit union but to participate in an afternoon with people from around the South Bronx, many of whom have been members of the credit union for years. The annual meeting, which is the members' principal opportunity to exercise their formal control over the credit union, was, in short, a process of community construction. It was not an exercise in participatory democracy or cooperative control.

As part of this case study, I conducted a mail survey of the membership of Bethex.[8] Among the respondents to the survey, who are probably more interested in the credit union than nonresponding members, there is little member participation in meetings and little sense of member control. More than 74 percent of the surveyed members said that they did not attend any Bethex meetings. Accordingly, members didn't even seem to know whether or not they have any control over the decisions made at the credit union (Table 5.1). This may reflect a passive contentment about Bethex on the part of its membership (and the results below suggest as much), rather than their complete estrangement and alienation from the credit union. And while the former is preferable to the latter, this is still not a model of member participation and community control.

Table 5.1 Members' Sense of Their Influence Over Decisions Made at Bethex

Responses	Percent
Don't know	57.1
Hardly any influence	6.5
A little influence	3.9
Some influence	19.5
A lot of influence	13.0

Capitalization

For much of its history, Bethex was capitalized entirely by its members' deposits. It received no nonmember deposits or grants for the first eighteen years of its existence, although it did receive equipment and supplies as donations from time to time. The first nonmember deposit came from St. James Episcopal Church, for $20,000 in 1988, which enabled Bethex to buy and maintain a computer. In the years since then, the size and role of nonmember deposits have grown significantly, and this increase has allowed the credit union to have a paid staff and to provide a much greater array of services to its membership. This has also meant that a decreasing portion of Bethex's assets come from its membership base, although it is still majority member capitalized. Currently, of the $3.5 million of Bethex's total deposits, about $2 million comes from its membership, with the remaining $1.5 million coming from nonmember deposits. Most of the largest (around $100,000) of these come from various banks and a few come from other credit unions. When the nonmember deposits are combined with the almost $500,000 in capital grants the credit union has received in recent years, member deposits only make up slightly more than 50 percent of Bethex's total assets.

Membership

Bethex's membership is not limited to the South Bronx but spread throughout the borough. The distribution within the South Bronx is also far from uniform, and the membership is, as would be expected, most concentrated in the Mount Hope area where the Bethex has been housed since 1993.

Outside the Bronx, there are substantial pockets in northern Manhattan (Harlem, East Harlem, and Washington Heights), and central Queens. Bethex also has members scattered throughout the rest of the country since, in the course of its thirty years in operation, many members have moved away but have not canceled their membership. Four percent of its membership lives outside the five boroughs, and 18 percent lives outside of the Bronx, in the rest of New York City. Despite the growth in membership over the last ten years, and the connections Bethex has made with other community institutions, the membership still seems to come to the credit union through rather informal social networks and channels. According to my survey, almost 65 percent of the credit union's members came to Bethex because a friend, family member, or coworker was already a member.

Loan Portfolio

Bethex's aggregate loan portfolio is relatively large by CDCU standards, hovering around $1,500,000 in total outstanding loans. Individual loans are typically modest in size and impact. The credit union currently has

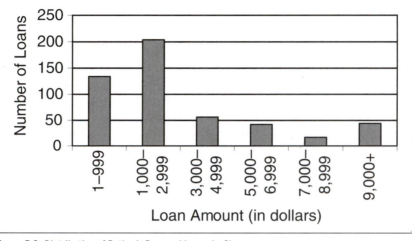

Figure 5.3 Distribution of Bethex's Personal Loans by Size

around 500 personal loans outstanding, with a mean loan size of $3,294, and a median loan size of $2,053. The median figure, as is often the case, is a truer representation of the CU loan portfolio, which is dominated by small-scale loans rarely for more than $3,000. This is reinforced by Bethex's policy that first-time borrowers cannot receive a loan for more than $3,000.

The loans tend to be consumer loans that allow borrowers the opportunity to buy household goods, repay debts (either to credit cards, family members, or loan sharks—and several loan applications listed the purpose of the loan as "repay loan shark"!), or invest in their countries of origin (see Table 5.2). Thus the lending is individual, largely consumer-based in character. Christmas loans, by far the most frequent type, are annual loans ranging from $700 to $800 made in November and December, with a fixed annual interest rate of 15 percent that is paid back over 12 months. The rest of the loans vary in size and terms, depending on the particulars of the member. The lending process at Bethex, as it is for most CDFIs, is a time-consuming and labor-intensive process, since many of the borrowers need to be educated about the basic processes of a loan transaction. Also, this means that loans need to be structured toward the needs of individual borrowers, and therefore the cost-savings that can be realized by the routinization of transactions occurs only with Christmas loans.

The demographics of Bethex's borrowers are also important to understand the role that its loans play. More than 65 percent of the borrowers are women. This reflects the predominance of women in the credit union's

Table 5.2 Distribution of Bethex's Loans by Type

Purpose	Percent
Christmas	24.2
Furniture/refurnish home	12.4
Pay Bills/debt/credit cards/rent/income taxes	11.7
Debt consolidation/build credit/build savings	9.7
Home purchase/repairs/improvement/moving	9.3
Buy/repair car	8.4
Travel/vacation/recreation	7.4
Send money to country of origin	5.1
Personal (unspecified)	4.4
Education	3.6
Business	2.9
Health problem/death in family	2.3
For family celebrations/holidays	1.4
Legal expenses/recover vehicles from pound	0.8
Help friends/family	0.6
To exhume a body	0.2

membership, a feature that has been part of the credit union throughout its history, and which, it should be added, is mirrored in its staff and board. The income of borrowers is equally important to understanding the role of the CU. The mean annual household income for borrowers is $18,972, while the median is $16,431. Bethex's borrowers are poor, but it is also predominantly not lending to the poorest of the poor (see Figure 5.4). Bethex does not document the race of its borrowers in any of its loan information.

Since the membership of Bethex is spread throughout much of the Bronx, to some of the other boroughs, and outside New York, it would make sense for its loan portfolio to reflect that dispersed geography, and this is certainly the case. Similar to the distribution of its membership, the largest concentration of loans is located in the Mount Hope area, although this concentration is much more pronounced for loan locations than for membership distribution. Individual borrowers, however, may or may not be investing the capital back into the Mount Hope area or even the South Bronx (Table 5.2).

Finally, the credit union also has a business loan portfolio, although, as is true for most CDCUs, it is much smaller than the personal loan portfolio. Bethex did not begin to make any business loans until 1989—and then it only did so because it was being pushed to by the NFCDCU and the requirements of a state grant. Business loans tend to be larger in size and

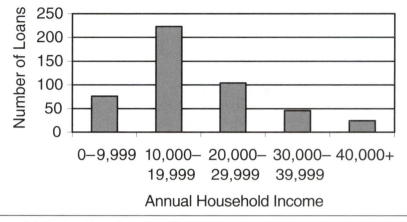

Figure 5.4 Number of Loans by Borrowers' Incomes

riskier than consumer loans, and, therefore, are much more time- and labor-consuming transactions. The business loan portfolio includes only about forty-five loans. The mean loan size is $11,983, and the median is $11,239. Bethex often works to help borrowers bundle different sources of capital together in order to meet their business's capital needs, which usually exceed the limited size of only $11,000. These loans go to start up, expand, or acquire various types of businesses, including self-employment, retail businesses, and services. The default rate on business loans is very low and almost all of the businesses repay their debts (although often not on time), and this is attributable, in part, to the thorough business planning that the credit union does with the borrowers before the loans are made.

Members' Satisfaction

The members of Bethex who responded to the survey were generally satisfied with the credit union. But the survey also reveals some of the problems with Bethex and with the credit-union model as a whole. Members were asked to rate their level of satisfaction with the credit union, and over 50 percent stated they were "completely satisfied" with the credit union, while only a combined 13 percent said they were "somewhat dissatisfied" or "completely dissatisfied." This measure may be biased, however, if those who responded to the survey were more likely to be happy with the credit union than the members who did not respond. A stronger measure of satisfaction, therefore, assesses how Bethex compares to the members' previous financial institution. When compared to prior financial institutions, the membership also rated Bethex favorably (Table 5.3). While this data

Table 5.3 Members' Satisfaction with Bethex Compared to Prior Institution

Responses	Percent
No previous financial institution	28.9
It's worse	12.1
About the same	22.9
It's better	36.1

suggests that the membership is happier with Bethex than with their prior financial institution, perhaps the most important finding here is that almost 30 percent of the credit union's membership hadn't banked anywhere else ever before. To some extent, the members are satisfied because they have not had any other options, and of the members who reported never having banked anywhere else before, over 80 percent stated they were "completed satisfied" with Bethex.

The members were also asked what they liked the most about Bethex and what they liked the least about it. A few things stood out in the results. First, members' responses were oriented toward the services provided by the credit union, and not toward its not-for-profit and cooperative structure. The credit union, this suggests, is—justifiably—primarily seen as a place where financial services are provided, and level of satisfaction is a function of its competency in providing those services. Accordingly, members' complaints were primarily over issues of service provision by the credit union, and they objected to the cramped space of its offices, its limited hours, etc. Second, having said this, a sizable minority of the membership liked characteristics of Bethex that stem from its cooperative structure. This is evident in the responses that addressed the credit union's concern for its members, its quarterly newsletter, and its annual meetings. Third, as I examined the results, I got the distinct impression that there were problems in race relations at the credit union. The objection of some of the members was that the credit union is almost entirely staffed by Latinas, and this runs counter to the demographics of the membership, which is a mix of African Americans, Latinos, Caribbean blacks, and whites. A typical comment was, "I don't speak Spanish and I am black. If you come there and you are not Spanish speaking, they take their time."

Members' Sense of Community

In a conversation about notions of community, Bethex board member Peter Bray stated: "Credit unions don't think as much about community or geography—they think of people and members." With this observation, he was recognizing one of the primary problems with CDCUS in general, and Bethex in particular: They are self-defined as community institutions and yet they operate at the level of the individual. Accordingly, there is little sense among the membership or the board that Bethex is a community. This is especially true among the newer members and board members (Peter Bray is a 1990s' addition to the board). Joy Cousminer and Elly Spangenberg both remember a strong sense of community when the credit union was connected to the Bethany Church and to the school for welfare recipients, but both acknowledge that the newer members do not share that history, and the credit union has not been able to connect them as community members. Spangenberg observed, "when I'm at the annual meeting, I get to see the members' children that have grown up with the credit union, and are now members themselves." And former board member Margaret Groarke stated at length, "I don't know how much I would [call Bethex's membership a community]. Every annual meeting I feel like it's a community, but that's what, one-thirtieth of our membership? That's pretty small. Being a member of Bethex is a link for some, and there are pockets within the membership like employees and long-term members. We are part of many communities but not one community. The long-term members are very much part of the credit union. The thing is, how big a community can you sustain? That group had to grow beyond its original base." The members themselves expressed a rather mixed sense of community, and when asked if they agree with the idea that being a member of Bethex made them part of a community, only 52 percent said they thought it did. The remaining 48 percent was fairly evenly split between those who did not think credit union membership meant belonging to a community, and those who had no opinion. Several members went on to ask, "What does Bethex have to do with the community?"

On the Potential and Limits of Collective Ownership of Money

Several conclusions can be drawn from this chapter—most of which will focus on Bethex and CDCUs. First, both LETS and CDCUs have grown dramatically and are viable organizational forms in the American political economy. Second, despite their viability, there are significant limitations to these models. CDCUs are rooted in the history of capital disinvestment by financial institutions, and these roots, which mobilize people to create alternatives, also severely constrain the prospects of those alternatives. This leaves CDCUs in the position of dependence on nonmember deposits and larger organizational member deposits to provide the assets necessary to run a financial institution. Bethex was able to *survive* solely on the capital owned by its members, but that survival was always very tenuous, and the organization was not able to grow and provide those members with anything more than a limited set of financial services. Local currencies can, theoretically, directly overcome this history of disinvestment—and it is commonly argued by LETS advocates that "a claim that a lack of money limits need being met is as unsustainable as a claim that houses cannot be built because there are not enough inches available" (North, 1999). But local currencies themselves suffer from issues of scale and scope. Simply put, if not enough people join the LETS, than the services available will be too limited to attract people to participate—or enable participants to use their scrip frequently. Similarly, even if participation is extensive within the locality, unless participating businesses produce sheetrock, plumbing, electrical wires, etc. (and produce them from local inputs), then it is unlikely that housing would be built without employing capital in the form of the national currency.

Third, while credit unions can be important institutions in improving the lives of their members, they are limited in their ability to improve the conditions of nonmembers in the places in which they are located. The loans are very small and consumer-based and therefore they are not able to dramatically transform places. Credit unions do bring capital into communities where it otherwise might not go (through nonmember deposits), and while they potentially keep capital in the community by lending only to their members, the problem of scale is ever-present. As one Bethex board member observed, "It's true of all low-income credit unions. On the one hand they're great, and do great things, but on the other hand they stink and it's because they think small." They do very little housing and mortgage lending (because of the size of those loans) and the business lending tends to promote microenterprise forms of self-employment. These kinds of businesses are not going to be generating employment for anyone other than the loan recipient herself. It is, therefore, unclear how much "local" development is stimulated by this model.

While the potential for local development is limited, CDCUs certainly improve the lives of their members. The members of Bethex reported being very satisfied with the credit union, and most stated it was an improvement over commercial banks. Similar to the experience with worker-ownership at Marland, this model of collective-ownership was able to serve a necessary purpose that would otherwise go unprovided by the structures and operations of the market. The evidence is fairly clear that Bethex serves a place, and a membership that for-profit banks have largely forsaken. Not only were almost 30 percent of Bethex's members unbanked before their membership, but the kinds of loans provided by the credit union are not going to be made at commercial and savings banks. To some extent, Bethex's "competition" for borrowers is not with banks, but with the other for-profit structures that have emerged in the context of banks' absence—loan sharks and check-cashing stores.

Fourth, the connections between local currencies or CDCUs and the places they are in can be relatively thin. Local currencies are place-defined, in that they can only be used in geographically delineated areas, but that does not necessarily mean that there are strong connections between the currencies and the places. And the connections of CDCUs to places are often even more tenuous. There are three sets of relationships that determine the connections between CDCUs and, to some extent, local currencies, and the places they are within. First, are the relationships between the CDCU or local currency and the sponsoring organization (in the case of Bethex, Bethany Church), and between the sponsoring organization and the other actors that constitute that place. Bethex was a credit union that, because it was kicked out by its sponsoring organization, manifested the mobility that is theoretically possible within this model. This mobility admittedly was very localized, and at no point did the credit union leave the South Bronx. Simply put, there remained some degree of local dependence, as Bethex could not relocate extralocally and remain Bethex. Second, the membership of credit unions is not place-bound, but membership is permanent, unless the member chooses to formally withdraw from the credit union. So as a credit union ages, its membership may, or may not, remain in the same place as the credit union. This is especially true for credit unions located in urban areas with high turnovers of residents and/or large immigrant populations, which can be very mobile. Third, collective ownership does not necessarily yield capital immobility or place dependence, as the loan portfolio of credit unions also does not need to be place-bound. Loans are made to members who have already relocated geographically, and members can use their loans for individual investments in places far removed from the credit union (e.g., to buy or repair a house in the Dominican Republic—the other side of global flows of capital investment are those associated with the transnational flows of labor). Granted this is a form of capital mobility that operates under a different motivation than for-profit investment capital seeking a "spatial fix" to improve the returns on its investment. But it remains a form of capital mobility nonetheless.

Fourth, this situation is further compounded by the individualized character of credit unions or the transactions in local currencies. The focus of a credit union is its membership, not its locality, and although these are intimately connected, they are clearly not synonymous—and, as was discussed in chapter 1, they would not be even if every resident in a locality was a member. Credit unions are peculiar cooperatives in that there is almost no involuntary interaction between members, and so a sense of shared experience or common identity is not constructed. In fact, credit unions legally have a very difficult time lending to "nonnatural" people (such as a not-for-profit corporation), and so connections between CDCUs and other local organizations are difficult to realize. If the common sense of localities is constructed through a layering of sets of experiences and relationships, then this layering is perhaps more difficult for credit unions than other kinds of organizations. That is not to say that Bethex has not constructed some of these layering relationships, and the connection to the public schools is a particularly powerful one. But the experience with Bethany church also highlights how tenuous these ties can be. Fifth, there is the issue of the nature of individualized monetary transactions. This is not only true for credit unions and their individualized lending decisions, but also true for local currencies. Money is an inherently alienating entity that requires an abstraction of understanding that creates distances in relationships. And while the level of abstraction in a local currency is clearly not what it is in a national currency, the introduction of money—rather than, say, informal barter or exchange—into the transaction depersonalizes the relations of those engaged in the transaction. Thus constructing community through monetary transactions seems to be contradictory in and of itself.

Finally, the linkages between the place and the credit union are further weakened by the lack of participatory democracy in the governance of the institution. This is not to say that Bethex, or other credit unions, is oppressive in its decision-making processes. But it is to say that control over Bethex is not distributed to a large number of actors in the Bronx. It is, in fact, a closely held set of controls, and the staff and board, while not inaccessible to the membership, make the decisions. Bethex is open, and the quarterly newsletters and the annual meetings can potentially remind the membership of their participation in something other than a bank, but the openness consistently remains at the level of informing the members, or at best, consulting with them (to borrow from Arnstein's [1969] ladder of participation).

The diffuse relationships between credit unions and localities is closely connected to the modest potential for credit unions to be a vehicle to realize local autonomy. And the question remains as to whether or not Bethex has empowered its membership, and the other local actors that constitute the South Bronx, vis-à-vis global capitalism. On some basic level, it has. The credit union is dependent on extralocal capital to be able to provide its services to its members. At the same time that it is dependent on nonmember deposits and capital grants, however, this reinvestment is controlled by the credit union's staff and board—and potentially, at least, by its members. This is reinvestment from without, but it is controlled from within.

To some extent, the issue of capital reinvestment is transformed by this model from a question of where the money comes from, to who controls the money once it is there. Admittedly foundations and financial institutions do not make investments or grants free of conditions and accountability, and the initiation of business lending at Bethex in order to receive a grant from the state is a powerful example of these conditions. But the credit union is still the institution that decides who receives the loans, and it can still lend money only to its members. There is, therefore, a degree of empowerment and autonomy in the processes of capital investment and the provision of financial services realized by Bethex and its membership.

The potential to use CDCUs as a component of localized oppositional struggles is also evident, but remains hidden and underexplored by those involved. The credit union's staff and board understands itself as doing something very different from for-profit financial institutions. This was made most clear to me in a conversation with a few staff members about an antiredlining activist in the Bronx. In this conversation, Ms. Cousminer observed, "The problem I have with [him] is that he doesn't think credit unions can fill in the holes left by banks. He thinks that banks don't lend to poor blacks because they're racist or whatever, and that they just need to be made accountable, and then they'll make those loans. But banks don't [refuse to] lend to poor people because they're bad people. They don't because it doesn't make sense to. Why would they? We can grow and fill in those holes. The problem isn't that banks are too big, it's that we're too small." Cousminer's argument reflects the conscious and reflexive recognition that what distinguishes CDCUs from banks is not size, but the logical frameworks under which they operate. This is a powerful understanding and contains within it potentially substantial political implications. This understanding, however, is politically underutilized.

The hypothetical growth of credit unions would not necessarily mean that they could offer the potential to transform the hegemony currently realized by for-profit financial institutions. There are two reasons for this. First, they are dependent on nonmember deposits, and those nonmember deposits often come from commercial banks. It is highly unlikely that those sources of capital would continue if CDCUs either politically presented themselves as counter-hegemonic or became large enough to offer a viable alternative. Second, CDCUs understand themselves largely in terms of opposition to banks. A commonly heard phrase is, "we bank the unbankable." This is a weak position from which to construct a new form of social practice, or new meanings of social relations to accompany that practice. It relies on the existence of the banks, and in doing so, reasserts the hegemonic position of those banks.

CDCUs and LETS are able to improve the lives of their members, and they provide some shelter for their localities from the vagaries of capital flows. In this way, they offer low-income people more autonomy over investment capital, and their own economic conditions and lives, than they would otherwise be able to realize. Beyond this, however, they are somewhat limited in their abilities to empower people to control their own localities and comparably constrained in their potential to work toward larger systemic change. Both deserve political and financial support because of the work that they do and the roles that they can play in the lives of low-income people and the trajectories of low-income communities. But we must also be realistic that because of both the inherent character of their work and the lack of a critical political context to embed that work, they face significant limitations in their emancipatory political potential.

CHAPTER 6

Conclusions

I began the research for this book by examining the organizations involved from the outside, largely from the perspective of the limited literature that has emerged in the last ten years to describe them. This literature, however, principally emanates from individuals who are writing to publicize and promote the organizations they describe. Particularly notable in this regard is Shuman's (1998) book *Going Local* which, on first reading presents a powerful set of arguments in support of exactly the kinds of localized collective ownership that this book has examined. He bases his arguments, however, on the points of view of the organizations themselves, a problem that hampers not only this smaller literature on localized collective ownership, but also much of the larger literature on community-based development in general. As a result of this bias, the conflicts, contradictions, and limitations of these organizations are often overlooked or downplayed. A similar problem can be found in Williamson, Imbroscio, and Alperovitz (2002) in their discussion of community-based economics—in what is otherwise an excellent book.

What this meant for me, as a politically committed researcher, was that I went into my fieldwork with a set of expectations about these organizations that probably were not justified. While I can appreciate the desire of people like Shuman and Williamson, Imbroscio and Alperovitz to promote groups that provide an alternative to the dominant local economic development orthodoxy (a goal I clearly support), these groups do not benefit from research that overstates their successes or their potential. The last thing these groups need is for outsiders to set them up to fail by creating sets of expectations that are not realistic and can never be met. Policy analysts less sympathetic than myself would, as I did, encounter the very real problems faced by groups trying to organize forms of collective-ownership and would judge them as failures based on the inflated expectations created by the advocacy literature. Finally, the extent to which these forms of ownership do actually constitute a viable and equitable alternative that allows for local control is exactly the empirical question I sought to answer in this book. And the answers are somewhat mixed.

The Viability of Collective Ownership

This discussion will begin with the basic question of: Is collective ownership a viable set of property and class relations in the current political economy? The answer to this question is yes, but not nearly as definitive a yes as might be assumed based solely on the recent proliferation of forms of collective ownership. The number of these organizations has grown dramatically in the last ten to fifteen years. This is because once these collectives are established, they are basically fiscally and economically viable. CDCUs possess financially sound portfolios and CDCU loan charge-off rates are in line with most other financial institutions. Limited-equity co-ops, CLTs, and MHAs are among the most fiscally frugal forms of affordable housing development, because the units are permanently affordable and do not need to be resubsidized. Worker-owned companies have repeatedly been shown to be more profitable than their traditionally owned competitors, and the more participatory the form of employee-ownership, the more profitable the company.

So to some extent, the question is answered in the affirmative. Collective ownership is a viable set of relations within the market. These are not hypothetical models, as real organizations have been created, and have demonstrated their viability. That does not mean that organizations do not collapse, or that worker-owned companies never go bankrupt. They clearly do. It does mean that when failures occur, it is not because of the model (collective ownership) that is being used, but instead it is one of the plethora of other reasons why failures sometimes occur in the trajectories of businesses and organizations.

This viability is significantly constrained, however, by the reliance on external support during the process of property acquisition or organizational growth. In several of the cases examined here—the Marland Mold buyout in Pittsfield, Mutual Housing in Stamford, and the land trust in Burlington—the collectives themselves *would not have existed* without financial assistance from the state as well private for-profit and not-for-profit institutions. In contrast, Bethex existed for almost two decades without any nonmember deposits or equity grants. But its existence was precarious, at best, as it continued to move from place to place with limited assets and a small membership base. The theme of "self-help" is a popular drumbeat in the dominant public sphere in American society, but, even in these extremely successful cases, it is exceptionally difficult to attain. Low-income localities, *by definition*, do not have the capital to directly, on their own, acquire the institutions that structure their relationships with the rest of the world. Extralocal capital is needed for these organizations to acquire the property or assets necessary for collective ownership to occur. And working with low-income people often further inhibits the ability of these collectives to realize self-sufficiency. CDCUs, for instance, struggle with the inherent inefficiencies involved in serving a low-income population—the high number of transactions relative to assets, the lack of financial literacy among their members, etc. The housing collectives also strain to provide housing that is simultaneously decent and well maintained, and affordable to low-income people. It could very reasonably be argued that such collectives need to exist because of the longer-term extraction of wealth from these communities—which has, in turn, played an important role in the accumulation of wealth by other people in other places. Thus the "outside" support is really a form of payback for the wealth extraction, rather than a form of charity—and that argument was made strongly by several Bethex board members. But such an argument is a necessarily political one, which is too often underutilized by the collectives themselves. And we will return to this issue shortly.

They therefore *may* be independently viable when they already exist, but they almost certainly cannot arrive at that juncture without outside investment. Their reliance on outside capital has significant implications not only for the viability of the collective-ownership model, but also for the prospects of using this model to realize local autonomy and as a component of larger social change.

Collective Ownership and Quality of Life

The forms of collective ownership discussed here seem to have substantially improved the quality of life for those involved. The residents/members/workers were genuinely satisfied with the organizations they were part of, and they all also reported that they are more satisfied with their current situation than they were before. This is, admittedly, hardly a scientifically derived conclusion, but the experiences and observations of those involved should be a central component of any analysis of organizations—especially when the projects are as small scale as these are. To some extent, the high levels of satisfaction reflect the lack of viable alternatives: If the workers don't buy the plant, they lose their jobs. Similarly, if the credit union isn't created, then many of the members have no access to loans or even checking and savings accounts. But this does not diminish the impacts of these organizations on the lives of those involved. In fact, the lack of alternative choices argues perhaps most powerfully for these forms of collective ownership. Collective ownership is needed precisely because the dominant structures of ownership simply were not willing or able to provide these people with the basic human needs of adequate housing, employment, and credit.

It was unclear, however, whether the organizations involved are able to equitably improve the lives of other people in the localities in which they are located. In the case of the worker-buyout, because the plant's economic linkages are extralocal, its ability to impact the lives of the rest of the people in Pittsfield has been limited. Similarly, Bethex's financial services, while being indisputably valuable to its members, are not able to improve conditions for the rest of the South Bronx. Both of these cases certainly have local multiplier effects, and the consumption enabled by these forms of collective ownership will have benefited some of the other people and businesses in these localities (and the joke at Bethex was that it was subsidizing the local furniture businesses, since so many of its loans were used by its members for the acquisition of furniture). But these impacts are still, given the small size of the collectives involved, rather limited. Mutual Housing in Stamford was able to improve the lives of other people in its locality more significantly than the other two cases, but this may have been through the successful organizing efforts of the residents, not necessarily the changed form of ownership and property relations. Of course, without the ownership structure, which both promoted resident organizing and prevented displacement, it is unlikely that such organizing would have occurred.

Collective Ownership and Local Autonomy

The basic question of this book, however, was the extent to which collective ownership allows local-scale actors to realize greater autonomy in their relationships with the rest of the world. The answers to this question are complex and varied and deserve the most attention here. To some extent, collective ownership does create a structure in which people in localities are in greater positions of control than they would otherwise be. The decisions made at these collectives are rooted to the places where they are. And the disconnections that can occur between mobile forms of capital, and the places where that capital needs to temporarily reside, simply do not take place. Accordingly, the possibility of uncontrollable flows of investment and disinvestment and the vagaries of the market are significantly mitigated by forms of collective ownership. Collective ownership, in short, provides localities with a shelter from the unjust demands of the market. Using, and significantly transforming, the language of Castells, collective ownership *can* reimbue place with some power as it forces place-based concerns into the structures and logic of the nominally place-less flows of capital.

The case of Marland is an excellent example of this, as the plant was to be closed not because it was unprofitable, but because it was not profitable *enough* to fit into the restructuring plans of Tredegar. The other cases indicate this as well, as the credit union, for all its mobility, was still functioning as a financial institution within the South Bronx through the 1970s and 1980s, a period when most private, for-profit, capital was fleeing from the area. And the creation of CHCA in the mid-1980s similarly provided stable and decent employment in the context of widespread unemployment and disinvestment. Similarly, the tenants of the different housing collectives all live with the security of knowing that their housing is not subject to disinvestment by a landlord (local or absentee), and that they will not be displaced by rapid increases in their rents when reinvestment in the form of gentrification occurs.

At the same time, however, these organizations face significant limitations as they work to mitigate the role of capital mobility on their localities. For while the market's logic is somewhat assuaged by the notions of community, locality, equity, and justice, these groups still exist within the market. Simply put, CHCA needs to be profitable in the market for home health-care workers in order to continue to exist—as the closure of Cooperative Home Care of Boston reminds us—and this reality necessarily dominates the corporation's thinking and actions. But this existence in the market is not only true for the collective ownership of places of work. As was discussed in chapter 4, both the CLT in Burlington and the MHA in Stamford have struggled with acquisition costs for potential new development because of increases in local property values—which themselves can be attributed, in part, to the successful work of the organizations. In short, these forms of collective ownership are *not* more "non-capitalism," despite some claims that they are (Gibson-Graham, 1996).

Their existence within capitalism brings with it a set of tensions and conflicts that these organizations must negotiate. To some extent they exist in both the realm of the market and the realm of agents for social change. This is not a position they can occupy for very long. The pressures of the market are very strong, both for the worker-owners, but also for the other collectives as well. But at the same time, the institutional support they need to survive is often provided by organizations (like the ICA) that see themselves as agents of social change and transformation. And so they are pulled in both directions. But these tensions run much deeper, as the interests of efficiency do not necessarily correspond with place-based concerns. And the goal of market efficiency often undermines the goal of organizing for social change. The collectives are thus constantly engaged in internal conflicts as they try to negotiate this "balancing act." This was most evident in the worker-buyout of the factory, for while local institutions played a central role in facilitating and negotiating the buyout, Marland Mold after the buyout was, in many ways, just another company in Pittsfield. The company responded to the needs of its shareholders and made its decisions accordingly. And although it has served as a model for other workers in the area, it has been somewhat passive in this regard. Another example of this comes from the evident tension in mutual housing between the development of new projects and the maintenance of a commitment to organizing the residents of the projects that have already been built. Finally, CDCUs must similarly balance the particular, and oftentimes, demanding credit needs of their low-income members, with the financial need to survive.

Existing within the market also means that for collectives other than worker-owned businesses, there is a consistent reliance on outside support. Simply put, private flows of investment do not result in adequate affordable housing or access to credit for low-income people, because these goals are not profitable. That is why the market doesn't provide them—although it's not quite that simple, as the racism of practices like redlining indicate that more than simple economic rationality is at work here—and that is also why these groups struggle to realize fiscal self-sufficiency. If the market could equitably provide the commodities being collectivized, then there would be little need for new forms of ownership to be created. These groups, because of their collective-ownership structures, operate with a logic that differs from the market. But it is clear that it is not quite that simple. Collectives that exist within the capitalist political economy (which is all of them) cannot simply will away the market's imperatives, but instead must find ways to operate simultaneously in the worlds of profitability and social change.

Also, communities and localities are never homogeneous and are always conflict-laden. And there is always a leap to go from the autonomy of a local organization to local autonomy of place. The relevant question is how large is that leap, and the more participatory and inclusive the organization, the smaller the leap. In this regard, there is much work to be done—even in these organizations that have received national recognition for their levels of participation and involvement. These collectives all suffered from a visible absence of participatory democracy in their governance. The management, staffs, and boards controlled the decision-making processes, rather than the workers, members, and residents. While the residents/members/workers are present on all the boards (and are the majority in mutual housing, and the worker- and resident-cooperatives), the board meetings I attended, and the interviews with the participants, indicate that their presence did not yield a process in which they were in positions of power. This is to some extent a function of the fact that most of the people involved were not too interested in democratically controlling their institutions. It also raises the messy question of the expectations that the collectives' owners would be involved in decisions to a far greater degree than most everyone else. It is politically unrealistic and morally suspect to advocate for frameworks for empowerment that unduly burden the low-income people and communities involved—people and communities with scarce amounts of time and resources. These collectives, in short, were not governed oppressively, but a dispersed ownership structure does not necessarily result in active, decentralized control.

But the potential for using collective ownership to realize local autonomy is not simply a function of localities being sheltered from the market, but that these forms of ownership would transform the meaning of their localities. Places are produced not only by flows of capital, but also by the experiences that occur within them and the ideological meanings attached to those experiences (how those experiences are "represented," to use Lefevbre's [1991] language). Places are partly produced by the "common sense" of those in them, and so local autonomy should be expressed through the transformation of the common sense of the place. The case study organizations have been somewhat less successful in this capacity than they have been in their market-shelter role. The most successful organization in altering the common sense of place was Mutual Housing in Stamford, which was able to organize and mobilize people to work to change the meaning and identity of the place.

The remaining cases were less evidently successful, although the experience of the workers at Marland Mold certainly did create a different, and much broader, framework for the enacting of economic and industrial policy in Pittsfield. The public sphere of the town was clearly shaped by the buyout process, and the success the company has realized since its workers acquired it. In this fairly traditional blue-collar industrial town, the notion of worker-ownership is now "on the table" when it otherwise would not have been. Bethex has largely failed in this capacity, and this is due to several factors: the limited size and public visibility of its loans and membership (although the partnerships with the schools have certainly helped in this regard); the individualized nature of the relationship between the credit union and its members; and the dispersal of its membership throughout the South Bronx (and upper Manhattan and Central Queens).

The principal barrier to local autonomy, however, might be a function of geographic scale and the characteristics inherent in the production of the local scale. Most simply, these are small organizations without the capacity to substantially address larger-scale social relations. The problem of scale, however, is not just a function of the empirical issue that these forms of ownership are small in size. It is also a function of the model of political change. These organizations are local organizations and therefore are not large enough to truly confront and transform the forms of capital that operate at larger scales. For while places might be the nodes through which flows of capital operate, the ability to access and control *a node* in *a place* is simply insufficient to effect larger change. If localities emerge, in part, out of the extralocal relationships in which they are embedded, then it is insufficient to try to control the production of localities solely at the local scale. Larger-scale structures of capital need to be confronted more directly than these localized collectives have the capacity to do. The multiplicity of the forms of capital also presents a problem for local autonomy. Capital is clearly not a unitary entity, but instead is a social process with a variety of manifestations and forms of accumulation. The chronologically simultaneous processes in Pittsfield of a localized collective being created at the same time that the local bank and newspaper were being acquired by larger-scale, extralocal companies exemplifies the reality of capital's diversity, and the problems that diversity poses for local autonomy.

Collective Ownership and Social Change

If the potential for local autonomy is mixed, then the political use of these forms of collectives is comparably difficult. There is the potential for these collectives to be a component of larger political struggles. They provide a framework for ownership that is both equitable and viable, but there are three principal barriers that must be overcome for this model to become part of a movement to challenge the hegemony of capital. These are: the lack of an oppositional politics by these collectives; the sources of the capital grants and loans they receive; and the disconnection from any political movement. I shall conclude by addressing these three issues.

The collectives examined in this book all emerged out of contradictions in the operations of capital. These were, however, local manifestations of those contradictions, and these responses have unfortunately remained at the local level. While the collectives involved tend to think of themselves as doing something different from the norm, they rarely go beyond that in their conceptions. These collectives are within the dominant framework, not simply because they respond to market forces, but because of how they understand themselves and the practices of their daily lives.

Ironically, this is the inverse of the political failures of the prior movements for collectives in the nineteenth century and 1960s. The political limits to those counter-institutions resulted from their desire to "opt out." This opting-out cut these institutions off not only from the dominant forms of capital, but also from those that were struggling against that dominance, leaving them politically marginal and unable to challenge capital. The current political shortcomings of localized collectives, conversely, results from being too much "within" the dominant framework of capital. In part this is because social structures are not a mountain that can be moved one rock, or social practice, at a time (to revisit the Maoist story of the 1960s). Instead the hegemony of capital is much more flexible and responsive. It also manifests itself in ways much more difficult to observe than a mountain is. The collectives might create new forms of ownership, but these practices exist side-by-side with a plethora of other social practices and meanings. It is therefore highly unlikely that one set of social practices different from the norm in people's daily lives is going to engender a radical transformation in people's understandings of the world and the meanings given to everyday activities. Local-scale alternatives, even if replicated, are not necessarily going to threaten capital's hegemony, unless they reflexively and consciously become local-scale oppositional struggles (and even then, they are still a long way from threatening capital). The contrast between social formations and practices that are oppositional and those that are simply alternative needs further exploring here. Raymond Williams has addressed these issues usefully and should be quoted at length:

> There is a simple theoretical distinction between alternative and oppositional, that is to say between someone who simply finds a different way to live and wishes to be left alone with it, and someone who finds a different way to live and wants to change society in that light. This is usually the difference between individual and small-group solutions to social crisis and those solutions which properly belong to political and ultimately revolutionary practice. But it is often a very narrow line, in reality, between alternative and oppositional. A meaning or a practice may be tolerated as a deviation, and yet still be seen only as another particular way to live. But as the necessary area of effective dominance extends, the meanings and practices can be seen by the dominant culture not merely as disregarding or despising it, but as challenging it (Williams, 1973, p. 11).

The political limitations of the current collectives is that they too often do not express the desire to use their experiences—both their crises in the market, and their successes in the collectives to transform social relations elsewhere. The members of most of the collectives do seem to recognize that they are involved in something different from the norm. But that does not necessarily mean they view themselves as doing anything politically significant. Because of this, even if these collectives continue to grow in number and public recognition, they are not likely to challenge capital unless the politics of those involved are transformed.

An important reason for the apparently limited politics of those involved is the source of capital for these organizations. These organizations rely on capital from without to acquire their assets or property. This capital comes primarily from the state and foundations, two sets of institutions that are rarely interested in funding local organizations that define themselves as oppositional to capital. These collectives are therefore left trying to "mainstream themselves" in order to receive capital. This desire to mainstream themselves in order to obtain capital raises a more fundamental question about the political potential of these groups. That is, they need extralocal capital because they acquire their property ("real" or otherwise) by buying it, and this acquisition process potentially reasserts the legitimacy of the hegemonic "buying and selling" of property framework. While I acknowledge that these collectives buy property because they have an immediate need for it (and can't "wait for the revolution"), there is certainly a different political meaning to a collective that chooses to squat on a property in order to remove it from the market, and one that chooses to buy that property in order to remove it from the market—which, again, is precisely why some of the squatters in the Lower East Side have chosen not to participate in the limited-equity co-ops there. In short, the model of property acquisition creates a situation in which these collectives have to mainstream themselves in order to obtain the capital necessary for that acquisition.

Finally, even if these organizations understood themselves as oppositional and chose extralegal forms of property acquisition, challenges to hegemony still require that localized struggles be waged as components of larger political struggles. The hegemony of capital, and the ability of certain forms of capital to move from place to place, and reproduce itself by infiltrating daily practices in different places, requires that oppositional movements organize simultaneously at the scale of both daily practices and the global economy. New social and spatial meanings can be created by new social and spatial practices, and alternative forms of ownership can be a central component of a larger political struggle, especially since their existence can provide the "objective" component of a "program" for change (to return to the Gramscian language this book began with). This cannot happen, however, if they exist in isolation from each other and any larger political movement. Just such a movement, at the global scale has emerged in the last few years. But, as will be discussed in the epilogue, it has done so largely disconnected from these localized collectives and their experiences.

The limitations notwithstanding, these collectives are unquestionably worthy of political support. Since the relationships between localities and the global economy are circular and reciprocal in producing this era of economic globalization and capital mobility, local scale actions still matter. And the efforts discussed in this book have demonstrated that localities *do* have options other than either passively suffering from capital mobility or actively acquiescing to that mobility. Local-scale actors can choose other directions, and there are more policy options available than might otherwise be readily apparent. But at the same time, there are clearly barriers to, and contradictions within, this model, and these barriers and contradictions need to be negotiated if it is to be part of a struggle to transform the dominant global political economy.

Our Resistance Must Be As *Local* As Capitalism

Place, Scale, and the Antiglobalization Protest Movement[1]

I was at the jail where a lot of protesters were being held and a big crowd of people was chanting 'This Is What Democracy Looks Like!' At first it sounded kind of nice. But then I thought: is this really what democracy looks like? Nobody here looks like me.
—Jinee Kim, Bay Area youth organizer (quoted in Martinez, 2000)

As should be clear from the preceding discussion, much of the political inability of the localized collectives to be anything more than simply alternatives comes from the lack of a systemic political critique in the larger community-development industry in which the collectives are located. But perhaps the collectives—and, for that matter, the more politically radical CDCs that do remain—need to look outside the community development industry for such a critique.

When the World Trade Organization met in Seattle at the end of November 1999, the occasion was marked by roughly 60,000 protestors representing a plethora of organizations and political and ideological goals. Their presence in Seattle made an immediate and important impact on American public life. Questions of trade and neoliberal globalization, which had been all but invisible in public discourse, became issues that were discussed and understood to be controversial. Since Seattle, protests have accompanied the meetings of the World Bank and International Monetary Fund, as well as the other global, and regional, institutions of global governance. Protests swept through the world since December 1999, from Bangkok to Washington to Chang Mai to Melbourne to Prague to

Nice to the Hague to Quebec City to Gothenburg and Genoa, and on from there, leading some commentators to call the year 2000, "the year of global protest" (Bello, 2001). There is certainly nothing new about protests and civil unrest over global neoliberalism and the institutions that promote and regulate it. And there are clearly echoes of both the antistructural adjustment food riots that exploded in the global south in the 1980s (Walton and Seddon, 1994) and the Chiapas uprising that began in 1994, shortly after the codification of NAFTA in North America. But the emerging sets of protests are both new and different because they transcend any particular locality or nation. The protestors have rallied around the theme of "our resistance must be as global as capitalism." This has been more than empty rhetoric. Instead it is a statement of both the organizers' goals, and an expression of the scale and form of organizing in which they are engaged. These are global sets of protests, and are accordingly organized at scales geographically larger than any locality or nation. And while this transcendence of smaller geographic scales offers the greatest potential of this new movement, it is also, I will argue here, somewhat problematic. In short, social movements need places in which to develop and prosper, and the privileging of the global scale over other, smaller, scales of organizing threatens to undercut the ability of the protests to realize the transformative changes that are its goals.

This epilogue has two primary parts. First, I will briefly discuss the methods of organizing that have created the emerging antiglobalization movement. Second, and the bulk of this chapter, will discuss the implications of these forms of organizing and the issues of place and geographic scale that they raise. Thus, while the bulk of this book has been about localized efforts in the global political economy, this final chapter shifts the focus to globalized efforts and their potential and limitations.

Scale and Organizing Against Neoliberal Globalization

The November–December, 1999, protests in Seattle marked the "coming-out party" for antiglobalization politics. But neither the organizing methods used nor the political coalitions evident in those protests were brand-new. Instead, both organizationally and politically, there are longer histories there. Organizationally, the Internet has played an incredibly important role in coordinating activities and serving as a forum for the exchange of ideas and information—and in many ways the Internet has been the central organizing mechanism for the antiglobalization protests. The potential of the Internet in antiglobalization organizing emerged in 1997, when a French environmental NGO revealed the details of the Multilateral Agreement on Investment (MAI), which had been negotiated in secret by the member countries of the Organisation for Economic Co-Operation and Development (OECD) since 1995. This release led to its distribution around the Web and a large coalition of NGOs opposed to the MAI emerged and eventually won their battle. This campaign, and not Seattle, marked the watershed for the Internet's use in antiglobalization politics. In the period since Seattle, the Internet has remained a vital forum for all facets of the organizing process, from the discussion of ideas, to the dissemination of information and the coordination of activities.

Similarly, the political coalition that emerged in Seattle was not new, but had built over the course of a decade. The environmental NGOs that came together to organize Seattle probably first emerged as a network in the buildup to the Earth Summit in Rio in 1992. And in 1994, the World Bank's fiftieth anniversary was met by a substantial network of groups that came together to form the "Fifty Years Is Enough" coalition—which continues to play an active role in this protest movement. Even the "blue-green" or "Teamsters-turtles" coalition, that so stunned commentators in Seattle has its roots in their common opposition to NAFTA in the early 1990s. Thus the often disparate groups of environmental organizations, trade unions, democratic-rights lobbies, and sustainable development groups had all been on the same side during one set of fights or another over the course of a decade. What was different about Seattle was not that these various groups were in oppositional agreement, but that they came together to protest and used the context of a major international meeting, and its attendant media focus, to do so.

In the various sets of protests that have come since Seattle, and have spread around the globe, large-scale NGOs and national-level unions have continued to be the central figures. Accordingly, the problems of globalization have therefore been constructed and understood by the large-scale NGOs, and the protestors, as global problems caused by multinational (or global) corporations and the global neoliberal public policies that promote and support them. They therefore need to be confronted on their own terms and at their own scale. We thus have a model of organizing in which large-scale groups use Internet-organized protests at multinational institutional gatherings as their primary vehicle for realizing social change.

Localized Efforts in the Antiglobalization Movement

This is not to say that there have not been other forms of organizing around more localized concerns, because that would be an oversimplification of things (and there is a great deal of diversity within the various organizations and actors involved). For instance, when the Bolivian government privatized the water supply to its city of Cochabamba, the price of water doubled almost immediately. In early 2000, the people of Cocha-bamba rebelled and took to the streets. They also, however, took to the In-ternet, and through its use, thousands of people around the world exerted pressure on the corporation (Bechtel Corporation). As a result of this local and global pressure, the company withdrew, and Bolivia renationalized the water supply to the city (Brecher, Costello, and Smith, 2000).

Another example comes from the growing movement to get large insti-tutional investors, like city governments and trade-union pension funds, to boycott the bonds that principally finance the World Bank. Already some large trade unions and several American city governments (San Francisco; Oakland, California; Milwaukee, Wisconsin) have agreed, as a result of local political pressure, to not invest in World Bank bonds. A sim-ilar movement is currently growing in both Britain and Continental Eu-rope (see Watkins and Danaher, 2001)—although state structures, their interscale relations, and pension-fund ownership and control probably limit the potential of this organizing strategy in Europe.

Some of the groups involved in the global protests have also been work-ing to integrate local and global organizing—and Jobs With Justice is cer-tainly notable in this regard. And a "Grassroots Globalization Network" has been created to promote local collectives in line with the antiglobaliza-tion protest movement's goals.

Also, I do not mean to imply that the protests have been devoid of local or community organizations, because that would also be too simple a de-scription. Perhaps the most visible American community organization in-volved in the antiglobalization protests has been the Kensington Welfare Rights Union from Philadelphia. Through its summer 1998 nationwide bus tour that ended at the United Nations, and its spearheading of the "Economic Human Rights Campaign," the KWRU had already become an organization that operated simultaneously on more than one scale when the protests erupted in Seattle. The KWRU was there, and also brought large numbers of people to the April 2000 protests in Washington.

But these examples, and the KWRU, stand out because of how excep-tional they are. In general, the current antiglobalization protests have been disconnected from organizing at the local and community scales. And community organizations have by-and-large stood on the sidelines and watched the protests from a distance (Axel-Lute, 2000).

Where Are/Were the Community Organizations?

To be fair to the antiglobalization protestors, the lack of connection to community organizations is not simply a one-way street or solely the fault of national and international NGOs organizing on the Internet. As would be suggested by the lengthy discussion in chapter 2, the lack of connections is also a function of how community organizations themselves have changed over the last thirty years. The lost social movement roots of community development—and the industry's acceptance of the neoliberal framework of small government and individualist, free-market solutions—are certainly partly to blame as well.

The political shift in community development is significant because, within the broad American community-development world, there are a host of social and institutional forms—those discussed in this book—that could have a radical political potential. But because of the larger, neoliberal, CDC political context in which they are embedded, that potential goes unrealized. The localized collectives discussed in this book all, in their own, individual ways, fit into the broad set of politics in which the antiglobalization protestors are interested. These are all, more or less, community-based, collectively owned, and democratically controlled by their members. They are therefore very powerful, if imperfect, examples of the potential for community control, economic self-determination, and meaningful economic democracy. But there is altogether too little interaction between these community-scale organizations and efforts, and the much larger-scale sets of protests.

The political implications of these disconnected scales of social organization, are significant and make up the remainder of this chapter.

Implications of Disconnected Scales

There are three primary reasons why, in order for the antiglobalization protests to become a social movement capable of transforming the global political economy, it needs to connect much more closely to local-scale politics and conflicts.

Place, Locality, and Social Movements

First, if we accept Mario Diani's broad definition of social movements as "networks of informal interactions between a plurality of individuals, groups and/or organizations, engaged in political or cultural conflicts, on the basis of shared collective identities" (Diani, 1992, p. 1), then the antiglobalization protestors need to pay closer attention to, and retheorize, local struggles.

On a simple level, this is because most people's daily lives, and their experiences of employment, home, school, etc., are still localized. And despite all the rhetoric and excitement about hypermobility, globalization, and transnationalism, most people still live in localized contexts and with predominantly local-scale sets of relationships and interactions.

But the fact that people's daily lives are still largely localized has vital political implications. Clarke and Kirby argue for an understanding of "locality as a nexus of community, household, and workplace, which are essential components of everyday life and crucial organizations that shape political values and ideology" (Clarke and Kirby, 1990, p. 394). The "shared collective identities" so crucial to social movement formation and development, can therefore never be fully divorced from the local scale of experience in people's lives. This is, in short, to restate one of the basic axioms in political organizing: You have to organize people where they're at—both figuratively and literally.

None of this is meant to suggest, however, that there are simple dichotomous pairs that exist between the local/global and experiential/abstract. Nor is it meant to suggest that such dichotomies would be synonymous or run in parallel. Instead, it is obviously recognized that systemic forces operate in and through a variety of geographic scales. Also, people's daily experiences, while localized, cannot fully be divorced from social interactions that take place in and through much larger scales (such as, putting on clothing made in China, drinking orange juice from Brazil, or watching the *Today Show* from New York or CNN from Atlanta). At their best, the antiglobalization protests' focus on systemic institutions demonstrate the interactions between global structures and people's daily experiences. And these protests have potentially opened a political space for antisystemic projects rooted in people's more localized experiences. In short, they have opened up the potential space for the collectives to define themselves as not simply alternative—but deliberately and reflexively oppositional.

But in acting solely at the global scale, the protestors ignore the reality that common, collective identities are rooted in, and shaped through, place-based experiences and struggles. As Naomi Klein, responding with disappointment to London's May Day 2001 protests, put it:

> There are clearly moments to demonstrate, but perhaps more importantly, there are moments to build the connections that make demonstration something more than theatre. There are clearly times when radicalism means standing up to the police, but there are many more times when it means talking to your neighbor" (Klein, 2001).

Also, the decision to prioritize international protests has very basic practical implications for local groups. Simply put, people and organizations in different places have varying amounts of political and financial resources that they can mobilize for any social-movement action. The emphasis on large protests focused at both the global scale and systemic level excludes most low-income organizations who lack either the financial resources to attend (or even to have widespread access to the Internet!), or the political luxury to focus on, and organize at, levels that are so much larger than their own daily struggles. One of the key critiques leveled against the antiglobalization protestors is that they are overwhelmingly white and middle-class. In a powerful assessment of the Seattle protests, which has been widely read within the protest movement, Elizabeth Martinez (Martinez, 2000) asked the simple question, "Where was the color in Seattle?" In her answer to that question, she inevitably comes back to the issues of the struggle being too divorced from the more immediate concerns of organizers in communities of color, and the racial disparities that characterize internet access.

Questions of Scale in Political Conflict

The second problem with the geographic disconnect between antiglobalization protests and local organizing efforts deals much more explicitly with issues of spatial scale. That is, the scale of any social relationship or social conflict is not a natural outcome of that social relationship. In fact it's not just an outcome at all, but instead it is both a constituent component in the production of the social relationship, and also an outcome of that social relationship. Geographic scales are socially constructed, and their social construction has powerful political implications. For instance, is the lack of affordable housing in New York a local problem (due to gentrification or the cost of land in the city), a problem of national government budget cuts, or a problem of the place of affordable housing in the global flows of investment capital? Well, it's a bit of all of those things. But how we understand the scale of the problem greatly influences how we organize to address it. Neil Smith has argued this point rather forcefully, and states:

> The construction of scale is not simply a spatial solidification of contested social forces and processes; the corollary also holds. Scale is an active progenitor of specific social processes . . . scale both contains social activity and at the same time provides an already partitioned geography within which social activity takes place. Scale demarcates the sites of social contest, the object as well as the resolution of contest (Smith, 1993, p. 101).

The antiglobalization protestors have done an amazing thing by reopening the global scale to contestation and challenge, and by insisting that neoliberal globalization—itself a political project deeply embedded in a politics of scale!—is not a done deal to which there are no alternatives.

But by privileging the global scale as the unit of analysis and realm of political organizing, the antiglobalization movement is overplaying its hand, so to speak. Conceptualizing local struggles as simply expressions or outcomes of larger-scale processes has four principal political implications. First, it conceptually devalues the importance of local political action. That is, if local situations are understood as just expressions of global,

Issues of local/global scale.

systemic processes, then to engage in local political action is to treat the symptom, rather than the cause. This, in turn, marginalizes localized struggles, and reinforces the gap between local and global struggles. This is an understanding of scale that is explicitly "nested." In it, actions taken at the global scale are understood to produce the outcomes of the smaller geographic scales. But as has been argued throughout this book, the global scale in no way exists prior to the local scale. And local scale actions and decisions are just as responsible for producing the global scale as they are products of it.

Second, it ironically accepts too much of the rhetoric of the transnational corporations, and multinational institutions that support them. In doing so, it erases the very real political, cultural, and economic differences between places. Globalization is not at all the same thing as homogenization. This is most clear in the rhetoric of "the race to the bottom" in which all the world's workers are thought to be moving toward a homogeneously impoverished level. This is both not empirically true (since the gaps between the North and the South are growing, not shrinking) and not particularly politically useful (since it denies the magnitude of the North-South divide—as well as divides between and within countries in both the North and the South).

Third, and similarly, not only does this privileging of the global scale accept too much of the multinational corporations' rhetoric, in terms of their views of scale as nested, but it also buys into their own framework of capital hypermobility and placelessness. But this is precisely the wrong understanding of globalization and mobility. Many forms of capital accumulation are a good deal less mobile than most of the rhetoric of hypermobility would have us believe. And even mobility requires going somewhere from somewhere else. Very few processes of capital accumulation exist in the ether, independent of real places, worksites, and neighborhoods. And the exploitation inherent in capitalism is not at all new, nor is it solely a function of capital mobility.

Finally, connecting with local-scale efforts will force the antiglobalization movement into the much more politically mature position of realizing that the "global" is not simply the aggregate of millions of "locals." That is, it cannot be assumed that local oppositional struggles will somehow just add up to a global opposition. If place matters in shaping how people live in, experience, and understand the world, then those place-based experiences and understandings can powerfully fracture and divide the movement—especially if there are not stronger linkages to various place-based struggles and conflicts. This is an extremely difficult and messy political reality that the movement must take very seriously.

All of this means that questions of geographic scale in the organizing of these protests must be reconceptualized. As David Harvey put it, "the choice of spatial scale is not 'either/or' but 'both/and' even though the latter entails confronting serious contradictions" (Harvey, 1998). For the protests to become a truly transformative social movement requires an explicit revaluation of local politics and the role of local struggles in producing the global political economy. In this way, the lessons from Cochabamba and the local World Bank bond boycott efforts are important. The Cochabamba effort was a successful example of using global-scale politics to transform a local political struggle. In this case, the scale of the conflict was transformed up by the organizers in Cochabamba who got the word out, and by the global activists who mobilized to put pressure on the company to withdraw. The local bond boycott effort explicitly addresses how the global scale can be an outcome of local-scale political fights. These are both examples of jumping scales in a local political fight, and connecting the local and the global, but the directions of causality are inverted.

Local Efforts and Building a Program for Social Change

The final reason why the anti-globalization protests need to connect much more closely with local organizing efforts relates to the ability to construct a program for social change. It is primarily at the local level, and often in the margins of the global political economy, what Michael Mann (1986) calls "interstitial locations," where new institutional forms are being created, experienced, realized, and learned from. Many of these new forms are in line with the broad political agendas of the protestors.

The antiglobalization protestors are currently facing the question struggled over by just about every oppositional movement in history. In short, this is, *How do you build from a language of resistance?* This question is further complicated by the tension that always exists in oppositional movements: Once they have decided upon a goal, or set of goals, does the movement stress the goals (the ends) or the movement itself (the means)? Closer linkages with local-scale alternative forms of ownership and control can help to address both of these key questions. This book began with a typically cryptic quote from Antonio Gramsci in which he argued that only through participating in the construction of a new hegemonic framework can aspiring counter-hegemonic projects realize their goals. There are decades of experience in constructing and maintaining forms of alternative, often oppositional, and potentially *counter-hegemonic*, forms of ownership and control in localities throughout the world, in both the global south and the global north. These experiences—and the conflicts, tensions, and contradictions evident in sober discussions of them—need to be part of the antiglobalization protest movement. They need, to return to the language of Gramsci, to be a central part of the program around which the antiglobalization protest movement builds and grows.

Conclusions

Over the short period of a few years, the antiglobalization protestors have used an explicitly global form of organizing to transform the public debate about neoliberalism and economic globalization. But the problem with the framework, and method of organizing, is that while capitalism is certainly global, and must be confronted as such, it is also most definitely local as well. And the exploitation and oppression that are part of neoliberal globalization, and which provide the moral and intellectual justification for the protests, are primarily felt at the local level. Despite this, it is clear that local and community organizations and organizers have largely passed on participating in the recent protests.

So while activists have constructed a forum to confront globalization, they have done so without incorporating the work of place-based organizers, who struggle to mobilize people, and keep people mobilized, in the face of local inequities. These organizers are needed in the fight against neoliberal globalization, and not simply because movements need places to find their strength and their expression (although they do), but because social change cannot be realized solely through periodic protests. As Juan Gonzalez (Gonzalez, 2000) wrote from Los Angeles at the protests that surrounded the Democratic National Committee's meeting there in August 2000, "The road to fundamental change in American society lies not simply in disrupting our downtowns, but in awakening, organizing and providing some vision of a better world to our South Centrals."

Notes

Introduction

1. By *neoliberalism* I don't mean the common American idea of a "liberal" as someone who believes in government intervention in the economy and who is broadly socially tolerant of diversity and difference. Instead, I mean the traditional meaning of the word "liberal" which is actually very different from its common American usage. A liberal, and neoliberalism as a political project, believes in very limited roles for government and in the priority of the individual and individualism over all else (like, for instance, community) in society. This project was clearly expressed by British Prime Minister Margaret Thatcher when she unapologetically exclaimed that, "there's no such thing as society, there are just individuals, who pay their taxes, and to whom we are accountable" (Young, 1988).
2. HUD defines this as a household that rents its unit, pays more than 50 percent of its total income in rent, and receives no public assistance.

Chapter 1

1. A slightly different form of this chapter was published in *Political Geography*. Reprinted from *Political Geography*, Vol. 18, James DeFilippis, "Alternatives to "The New Urban Politics": finding locality and autonomy in local economic development," pp. 973–990, 1999, with permission from Elsevier.
2. This title comes from the name of John Maynard Keynes, the Cambridge University economist that was instrumental in the creation of the welfare state in the Western world.
3. They are, of course, correct and are stating the very basis of this book. Unfortunately, they do not follow their own observations to their logical conclusions.
4. Perhaps the best evidence of this transformation is the 1995 addition of 'concern for community' to the principles adhered to by the International Cooperative Alliance (Hoyt, 1996).

Chapter 2

1. The title of this section subheading is taken from the title of Smith and Lipsky's 1993 book.

Chapter 3

1. *Congressional Record*, 97th Congress, 1st Session, 1981, 127, no. 72.
2. quoted in Russell, 1984.

3. "Fordist" refers to the system of large-scale industrial production that dominated the American economy for most of the twentieth century. The name, of course, comes from Henry Ford, who created the assembly line, which became the model for how to organize a modern industrial facility and firm.

4. Does not include employment in the Finance, Insurance, Real Estate (FIRE) sectors, or Wholesale and Retail Trade, which grew by 45 percent and 38 percent, respectively, over this same twenty-year period.

5. When a nonleveraged ESOP is established, it is usually not with the intent of having the employees own a majority or all of the firms' shares. Instead it is used by companies who wish to "donate" shares to their employees—usually to prevent hostile takeovers or realize the tax benefits associated with ESOPs (Megson and O'Toole, 1993).

6. This cut in funding has led to the closure of 20 percent of the home-care service providers in the years since 1997 (Inserra, Conway, and Rodat, 2002).

7. This discussion is based on Nash's (1989) excellent history of the city. Her book, which reads like one of the "community studies" of the 1950s and 1960s, is actually much more sophisticated than what people usually associate with that literature. It is a local history, but it is very attuned to the place of that locality in the larger political economy, and the important role of the political economy in partially constituting that local history.

8. Through 1992, there was a progression as the popular press (and the workers quoted therein) began to change how they referred to the plant from Tredegar Molded to Marland Mold.

9. When I am quoting workers from the interviews, they will remain nameless.

10. This problem was made abundantly clear in the case of Enron, which was a minority worker-owned firm, whose bankruptcy left many of its workers with no jobs and no real source of retirement income and wealth.

11. Unfortunately, the plant closed. The efforts to keep it open were too late in coming and it was unclear whether or not the plant was viable at all.

Chapter 4

1. For more thorough discussion and evidence, see: National Low Income Housing Coalition, 1999; National Low Income Housing Coalition, 2000; State of Low Income Housing, 2000; State of the Nation's Housing, 1999; Stegman, Quercia, and McCarthy, 2000; U.S. Department of Housing and Urban Development, 2000; US Department of Housing and Urban Development, 2000a

2. Defined as an unsubsidized household that rents and pays more than half its income in housing costs or lives in severely inadequate housing.

3. Defined as a household that pays more than half its income in housing costs or lives in severely inadequate housing.

4. Cooperatives are almost exclusively found in multi-unit buildings, rather than developments with single-family homes.

5. And this was certainly the representation of the squatters in the most popular depiction of them, the Broadway play *Rent.*

6. The project-based Section 8 housing stock was built with low-income requirements that the private owners can "opt out" of after 20 years. Thus there has been a significant loss of these affordable units in recent years, as owners have increasingly opted-out of the program.

7. The federal program created in 1986 allows developers of low-income housing to receive credits for their taxes, provided they maintain the housing as affordable to low-income people. In practice, the developers, which are predominantly not-for-profit corporations, form partnerships with equity investors that are for-profit entities that, in turn, receive the tax credits to offset taxes they would otherwise owe. It is, by far, the largest type of federal subsidies for affordable housing.

Chapter 5

1. Bretton Woods was one of the primary economic institutions created at the end of World War II. In it, the American dollar was the global standard by which all other currencies had

their value weighed. Its collapse in the early 1970s meant that currencies are no longer tied to anything, are free-floating, and their relative values are shaped by the global market for them.

2. Income in Figure 1 and Figure 2 is grouped according to median household income in a zip code relative to the median household income for the metropolitan statistical area (MSA) in which the zip code is located. Low income is a zip code with less than 50 percent of the area's median. For moderate income, it is 50–80 percent. For middle income it is 80–120 percent, and for high income, it is more than 120 percent of the area's median.

3. Redlining gets its name, however, not from banks directly but from the practices of the Federal Housing Administration (FHA), and it was their practice of drawing red lines around nonwhite neighborhoods and denying insurance to them that has given this powerful form of racism its name.

4. Defined as the difference between families' gross assets and their liabilities.

5. In many ways, the early credit unions (and credit unions today) perform the same function as the old immigrant mutual savings and loan associations, which were different from most savings and loans in that they were owned by their depositors and borrowers (most S&Ls are owned by shareholders, see Parzen and Kieschnick, 1992)—and the images of George Bailey in *It's A Wonderful Life* reflect the importance of these institutions to immigrants like Frank Capra (Mangione and Morreale, 1993).

6. Low Income Credit Unions (LICU) are designated by the NCUA based on the incomes of their members, and while LICUs are not synonymous with CDCUs, the vast majority of LICUs are also CDCUs (Williams, 1998).

7. The name Bethex comes from the Bethany Church, but since the organizers had grand ambitions for the credit union, they called it "Bethex" because "all the big companies like Amex and FedEx end in 'ex.' " (Cousminer, 1998–99)

8. I sent survey instruments in Spanish and English to a randomly selected 10 percent of the credit union's members (570 members), and I received back a total of 92 completed questionnaires, yielding a response rate of 16.14 percent. While this was a worse response rate than I had hoped for, and the members had been notified in advance about the survey in Bethex's newsletter, this fairly low response rate is suggestive of the limited relationship most members have with the credit union.

Epilogue

1. Previously published as "Our Resistance Must Be as *Local* as Capitalism: Place, Scale and the Anti-Globalization Protest Movement" in *City: Analysis of Urban Trends, Culture, Theory, Policy, Action*, 5(3): 363–373.

Bibliography

Adams, F. and G. Hansen. 1992. *Putting Democracy to Work.* 2nd Ed. San Francisco: Berrett-Koehler Publishers.

Agnew, J. 1987. *Place and Politics: the Geographical Mediation of State and Society.* Boston: Allen and Unwin.

Alinsky, S. 1969 (1946). *Reveille for Radicals.* New York: Random House.

Allen, L. 1969. Making capitalism work in the ghettos. *Harvard Business Review,* May–June: 83–92.

Alshuler, A. 1970. *Community Control.* New York: Pegasus.

American Federation of State, County and Municipal Employees. 2001. *Cheating Dignity.* Washington, D.C.

Arendt, H. 1958. *The Human Condition.* Chicago: University of Chicago Press.

Arrighi, G. 1994. *The Long Twentieth Century.* London: Verso.

Avery R., R. Bostic, P. Calem, G. Canner. 1997. Changes in the distribution of banking offices. *Federal Reserve Bulletin,* September: 707–725.

Axel-Lute, M. 2000. Back to the streets: Why community developers should join the fight against corporate globalization. *Shelterforce,* May/June: 14–19.

Beauregard, Robert. 1993. *Voices of Decline.* Cambridge, MA: Blackwell.

Bello, W. 2001. 2000: the year of global protest. *International Socialism,* spring: 71–77.

Bendick, M. and M. L. Egan. 1991. *Business Development in the Inner-City: Enterprise with Community Links.* New York: Community Development Research Center/New School for Social Research.

Benello, C. G. 1992. *From the Ground Up.* L. Krimmerman, F. Lindenfield, C. Karty, and J. Benello (eds.). Boston: South End Press.

Benello, C. G. and D. Roussopoulos (eds.). 1971. *The Case For Participatory Democracy: Some Prospects for a Radical Society.* New York: Grossman Publishers.

Berger, R. and C. Steinbach. 1992. *A Place in the Marketplace: Making Capitalism Work in Poor Communities.* Washington, D.C.: National Congress for Community Economic Development.

Berkowitz M. 1997. Not So "Natural." *What You Need To Know: Technical Information for Community Development Credit Unions,* April: 1–2.

Berkshire Eagle. 1992. Localism, protectionism and free trade. 24 August.

Berndt, H. E. 1977. *New Rulers in the Ghetto: The Community Development Corporation and Urban Poverty.* Westport, CT: Greenwood Press.

Blakely, E. J. and L. Small. 1996. Michael Porter: New Gilder of Ghettos. Review of Black Political Economy. Fall/Winter, 161–183.

Bluestone, B. and B. Harrison, 1982. *The Deindustrialization of America.* New York: Basic Books.

Boggs, J. 1970. *Racism and the Class Struggle.* New York: Monthly Review Press.

Bowe, S. 2000. Payday loan stores accused of preying on America's poor. *Financial Times*, 23 February.

Boyte, H. 1980. *The Backyard Revolution: Understanding the New Citizen Movement.* Philadelphia: Temple University Press.

Bray, P. 1999. Board Member, Bethex Federal Credit Union, personal interview, February.

Brecher, J. and T. Costello. 1994. *Global Village or Global Pillage: Economic Reconstruction from the Bottom Up.* Boston: South End Press.

Brecher, J., T. Costello, and B. Smith. 2000. *Globalization from Below.* Boston: South End Press.

Brown, M. 1992. The possibility of local autonomy. *Urban Geography*, 13: 257–279.

Browne L. E. and G. Tootell. 1995. Mortgage lending in Boston—A response to the critics. *New England Economic Review*, Sep–Oct: 53–78.

Bruyn, S. T. and J. Meehan (eds.). 1987. *Beyond the Market and the State: New Directions in Community Development.* Philadelphia: Temple University Press.

Carmichael, S. and C. V. Hamilton. 1967. *Black Power.* New York: Vintage.

Carr, James. 1999. Community, Capital and Markets: A New Paradigm for Community Reinvestment. *The Neighborworks Journal*, summer: 20–23.

Castells, M. 1977. *The Urban Question: A Marxist Approach.* London: Edward Arnold.

———. 1983. *The City and the Grassroots.* Berkeley: University of California Press.

Clark, G. 1984. A theory of local autonomy. *Annals of the Association of American Geographers*, 74: 195–208.

———. 1989. *Unions and Communities Under Siege.* Cambridge, UK: Cambridge University Press.

Clarke, S. 1990. Precious place: the local growth machine in an era of global restructuring. *Urban Geography*, 11: 185–193.

———. 1993. The profound and the mundane: analyzing local economic development activities. *Urban Geography*, 14: 78–94.

Clarke, S. and A. Kirby. 1990. In search of the corpse: The mysterious case of local politics. *Urban Affairs Quarterly*, 25: 389–412.

Clarke, S. and G. Gaile. 1998. *The Work of Cities.* Minneapolis: University of Minnesota Press.

Clavel, P. 1986. *The Progressive City.* New Brunswick, NJ: Rutgers University Press.

Collins, C., C. Hartman, and H. Sklar. 1999. *Divided Decade: Economic Disparity at the Century's Turn.* United for a Fair Economy. Boston: United for a Fair Economy.

Congressional Budget Office. 2001. *Historical Effective Tax Rates, 1979–1997: Preliminary Edition.* Washington, D.C.

Conroy, W. J. 1990. *Challenging the Boundaries of Reform: Socialism in Burlington.* Philadelphia: Temple University Press.

Cooperative Home Care Associates. 2002. *Fact Sheet.* Bronx, NY.

Cousminer J. 1998–9. Treasurer/Manager, Bethex Federal Credit Union. Personal and telephone interviews, July–July.

Cox, K. 1993. The local and the global in the new urban politics: a critical view. *Environment and Planning D: Society and Space*, 11: 433–448.

———. 1995. Globalisation, competition and the politics of local economic development. *Urban Studies*, 32(2): 213–224.

———. 1997. Introduction: Globalization and its politics in question. In K. Cox (ed.). *Spaces of Globalization: Reasserting the Power of the Local.* New York: Guilford Press.

Cox, K. and A. Mair. 1988. Locality and community in the politics of local economic development. *Annals of the Association of American Geographers*, 78(2): 307–325.

———. 1989. Levels of abstraction in locality studies. *Antipode*, 21(2): 121–132.

Cruse, H. 1969. *Rebellion or Revolution.* New York: Apollo Books.

Davis, J. E. (ed.) 1994. *The Affordable City: Toward a Third Sector Housing Policy.* Philadelphia: Temple University Press.

de Souza Briggs, X., E. Mueller, and M. Sullivan. 1997. *From Neighborhoods to Communities: The Social Impacts of Community Development Corporations.* New York: Community Development Research Center New School for Social Research.

de Tocqueville, Alexis. 1969 (1835). *Democracy in America.* J. P. Mayer (ed.) George Lawrence (trans.) Garden City, NY: Doubleday.

Deasy, J. 1998. executive director, Manhattan Borough Development Corporation. Personal interview, 24 June.

DeFilippis, J. 1997. Community, locality, and the transformation of inter-scale relations in the American political economy. Paper presented at the Annual Meeting of the Political Geography Specialty Group of the Association of American Geographers. San Marcos, TX. April.

———. 1999. Alternatives to the "New Urban Politics": finding locality and autonomy in local economic development. *Political Geography* 18: 973–990.

———. 2001. The myth of social capital in community development. *Housing Policy Debate.* 12(4): 781–806.

———. 2002. Equity vs. equity: Property reform and community control in the U.S. *Local Economy.* 17(2): 149–153.

Delgado, G. 1986. *Organizing the Movement: The Roots and Growth of ACORN.* Philadelphia: Temple University Press.

Di Domenico, J. 1999. Loan Officer, Bethex Federal Credit Union. Personal interview, April.

Diani, M. 1992. The concept of social movement. *The Sociological Review* 40: 1–25.

Dicken, Peter. 1998. *Global Shift: Transforming the Global Economy,* 3rd ed. Thousand Oaks, CA: Sage.

DiGiovanna, S. 1997. *Fighting for a Working Future: Emerging Models of Local Union Strategy in a New Era of Global Competition.* Ph.D. Thesis. Toronto: Graduate Department of Geography, University of Toronto.

Douthwaite, R. 1996. *Short Circuit: Strengthening Local Economies for Security in an Unstable World.* Dublin, Ireland: The Lilliput Press.

Doyle, J., J. Lopez, and M. Saidenberg. 1998. How effective is lifeline banking in assisting the 'unbanked'? *Current Issues in Economics and Finance* 4 (6): 1–6.

Dworkin, G. 1988. *The Theory and Practice of Autonomy.* Cambridge, UK: Cambridge University Press.

Dymski, G. and J. Veitch. 1996. Financial transformation and the metropolis: booms, busts, and banking in Los Angeles. *Environment and Planning A,* 28: 1232–1269.

Economist, The. 2000. The case for globalisation. 23 September.

Economist, The. 2002. Crisis? What crisis? May 16.

Eichler, M. 1998. Look to the future, learn from the past. *Shelterforce Online,* September/October. http://www.nhi.org/online/issues/101/eichler.html

Eisinger, P. 1998. City politics in an era of federal devolution. *Urban Affairs Review,* 33(3): 308–325.

Epstein, R. 1996. The de-activist. *City Limits,* October: 18–23.

Fainstein, N. and S. Fainstein. 1976. The future of community control. *The American Political Science Review* 70: 905–923.

Fainstein, S. 1987. Local mobilization and economic discontent. In M.P. Smith and J. Feagin (eds.). *The Capitalist City.* Cambridge, MA: Blackwell.

Faux, G. 1971. *CDCs: New Hope for the Inner City.* New York: Twentieth Century Fund.

Ferrer, F. 1998. *Risen From The Ashes: An All-America City Plans Its Future: Strategic Policy Statement for The Bronx.* Bronx, NY: Bronx Borough President's Office.

Fish, J. H. 1973. *Black Power, White Control: The Struggle of the Woodlawn Organization in Chicago.* Princeton, NJ: Princeton University Press.

Fisher, R. 1994. *Let The People Decide: Neighborhood Organizing in America, Updated Edition.* New York: Twayne Publishers.

Foucault, M. 1980. *Power/Knowledge.* C. Gordon (ed. and trans.) New York: Pantheon.

Fox, J. A. 1998. The growth of legal loan sharking: A report on the payday Loan Industry. Consumer Federal of America Web page, http://www.stateandlocal.org/loanshar.html, accessed February 2000.

Friedman, M. 1970. The social responsibility of business is to increase its profits. *New York Times Magazine,* 13 September.

Fulton, W. 1987. Off the barricades, into the boardrooms. *Planning,* August: 11–15.

Furdell, P. 1994. *Poverty and Economic Development: Views of City Hall.* Washington, D.C.: National League of Cities.

Giddens, A. 1979. *Central Problems in Social Theory: Action, Structure and Contradiction in Social Analysis.* London: Macmillan.

Gittell, M. 1980. *The Limits to Citizen Participation: The Decline of Community Organizations.* Beverly Hills, CA: Sage.

Gittell, R. and A. Vidal. 1998. *Community Organizing: Building Social as a Development Strategy.* Thousand Oaks, CA: Sage.

Goetz, E. and S. Clarke (eds.). 1993. *The New Localism: Comparative Urban Politics in a Global Era.* Newbury Park, CA: Sage.

Gonzalez, J. (2000) From Seattle to South Central. *In These Times*, 18 September.

Goozner, M. 2000. Blinded by the boom: What's missing in the coverage of the New Economy? *Columbia Journalism Review*, Nov/Dec.

Gottdiener, M. 1986. *The Decline of Urban Politics: Political Theory and the Crisis of the Local State.* Newbury Park, CA: Sage.

Gramsci, A. 1971. *Selections from the Prison Notebooks.* Q. Hoare and G. N. Smith (ed. and trans.). New York: International Publishers.

Green, G. and G. Faux. 1969. The social utility of black nterprise. In W. Haddad and D. Pugh (eds.). *Black Economic Development.* Englewood Cliffs, NJ: Prentice Hall.

Groarke, M. 1999. Former board member and chair of the Supervisory Committee of Bethex Federal Credit Union. Telephone interview, May.

Grogan, P. and T. Proscio. 2000. *Comeback Cities.* New York: Westview Press.

Gunn, C. 1992. Plywood co-operatives in the United States. *Economic and Industrial Democracy* 13: 525–534.

Gunn, C. and H. Gunn. 1991. *Reclaiming Capital: Democratic Initiatives and Community Development.* Ithaca, NY: Cornell University Press.

Gurr, T. and T. King. 1987. *The State and the City.* Chicago: University of Chicago Press.

Hall, T. and P. Hubbard. 1996. The entrepreneurial city: new urban politics, new urban geographies? *Progress in Human Geography* 20(2): 153–174.

———. 1998. *The Entrepreneurial City: Geographies of politics, regime and representation.* New York: Wiley.

Halpern, R. 1995. *Rebuilding the Inner City: A History of Neighborhood Initiatives to Address Poverty in the United States.* New York: Columbia University Press.

Hanna, Timothy. 2002. Retail Fees of Depository Institutions, 1997–2001. *Federal Reserve Bulletin*, September: 405–413.

Harrison, B. and B. Bluestone. 1988. *The Great U-Turn: Corporate Restructuring and the Polarizing of America.* New York: Basic Books.

Hartman, C. 2001. Income patterns: Facts and figures. On Inequality.org.: http://www.inequality.org/facts3fr.html, accessed June 10, 2002.

Harvey, D. 1989. *The Condition of Post-Modernity.* Cambridge, MA: Blackwell.

———. 1989a. From managerialism to entrepreneurialism: The transformation of urban governance in late capitalism. *Geografiska Annaler* 71(B): 3–17.

———. 1996. *Justice, Nature and the Geography of Difference.* Oxford: Blackwell.

———. 1998. The geography of class power. In L. Panitch and C. Leys (eds.). *The Communist Manifesto Now: Socialist Register 1998.* New York: Monthly Review Press.

Hawke, J. 2002. Community Development Financial Institutions and CD banks—natural partners for traditional lenders. *Community Developments: The OCC's Community Affairs Newsletter.* summer.

Herbert, B. 2001. Championing cities. *New York Times*, April 26.

Hirst, P. and G. Thompson. 1996. *Globalization in Question.* Cambridge: Polity Press.

Hogarth, J. and K. O'Donnell. 1999. Banking relationships of lower-income families and the governmental trend toward electronic payment. *Federal Reserve Bulletin*, July: 459–473.

Horowitz, C. 1994. A South Bronx renaissance. *New York* 27(46): 54–59.

Imbroscio, D. 1997. *Reconstructing City Politics: Alternative Economic Development and Urban Regimes.* Thousand Oaks, CA: Sage.

Immergluck, D. 1999. Fishing for herring? Comments on 'redlining or red herring?' In J. Gunther, K. Klemme, and K. Robinson (eds.). Federal Reserve Bank of Dallas Woodstock Institute Web page, http://www.nonprofit.net/woodstock/dallasfed.html, accessed February 2000.

Innis, R. Separatist Economics: A New Social Contract. In W.F. Haddah and G.D. Pugh (eds.). *Black Economic Development.* Englewood Cliffs, NJ: Prentice Hall.

Inserra, A., M. Conway, and J. Rodat. 2002. *Cooperative Home Care Associates: A Case Study of a Sectoral Employment Development Approach.* Washington, D.C.: Aspen Institute.

Jessop, B. 1990. *State Theory: Putting Capitalist States in Their Place.* University Park: Penn State University Press.

Jones, D. J. 1979. Not in my community: The neighborhood movement and institutionalized racism. *Social Policy* 10(2): 44–47.

José, V. C. 1989. A South Bronx landscape. *The Nation*, 6 March: 302–306.

Kain, J. F. and J. J. Persky. 1971. Alternatives to the gilded ghetto. In R. W. Bailey (ed.). *Black Business Enterprise: Historical and Contemporary Perspectives.* New York: Basic Books.

Kanter, R. M. 1995. *World Class.* New York: Simon and Schuster.

Kantor, P., with S. David. 1988. *The Dependent City.* Glenview, IL: Scott, Foresman.

Kantor, Paul. 1995. *The Dependent City Revisited.* Boulder, CO: Westview.

Katz, Cindi. 1995. Major/minor: Theory, nature, and politics. *Annals of the Association of American Geographers* 85(1): 164–167.

Katznelson, I. 1981. *City Trenches: Urban Politics and the Patterning of Class in the United States.* Chicago: University of Chicago Press.

Kelly, R. M. 1977. *Community Control of Economic Development.* New York: Praeger.

Kennickell, A., M. Starr-McCluer, and B. Surette. 2000. Recent changes in U.S. family finances: Results from the 1998 survey of consumer finances. *Federal Reserve Bulletin,* January: 1–29.

Kincaid, J. 1997. *American Cities in the Global Economy.* Washington, D.C.: National League of Cities.

Klein, N. 2001. May Day's lessons for the rootless, *Guardian,* 3 May.

Kolodny, R. 1987. The emergence of self-help as a housing strategy for the urban poor. In R. Bratt, C. Hartman, and A. Meyerson (eds.). *Critical Perspectives on Housing.* Philadelphia: Temple University Press.

Kotler, M. 1969. *Neighborhood Government: The Local Foundations of Political Life.* Indianapolis, IN: Bobbs-Merrill Company.

———. 1971. The Politics of Community Economic Development. *Law and Contemporary Problems* 36: 3–12.

Kretzmann, J. and J. McKnight. 1993. *Building Communities from the Inside Out: A Path Toward Finding and Mobilizing a Community's Assets.* Chicago: ACTA Publications.

Krimmerman, L. 1999. The Uncertain Future of Worker Ownership: Two Decades of Lessons. *Planners Network.* May/June.

Krinsky, J. and S. Hovde. 1996. *Balancing Acts: The Experience of Mutual Housing Associations and Land Trusts in Urban Neighborhoods.* New York: Community Service Society of New York.

Lake, R. 1994. Negotiating local autonomy. *Political Geography,* 13: 423–442.

Lang, R. and S. Hornburg. 1998. What is social capital and why is it important to public policy? *Housing Policy Debate* 9(1): 1–16.

Lash, S. and J. Urry. 1987. *The End of Organized Capitalism.* Madison: University of Wisconsin Press.

Leavitt, J. and S. Saegert. 1990. *From Abandonment to Hope: Community-Households in Harlem.* New York: Columbia University Press.

Lee, R. and J. Wills (eds.). 1999. *Geographies of Economies.* New York: Arnold.

Lefebvre, H. 1991 (1974). *The Production of Space.* D. Nicholson-Smith (trans.). Oxford: Blackwell.

Leitner, H. 1990. Cities in pursuit of economic growth: the local state as entrepreneur. *Political Geography Quarterly* 9(2): 146–170.

Lenz, T. 1988. Neighborhood development: Issues and models. *Social Policy,* spring: 24–30.

Lietaer, B. 2001. *The Future of Money.* London: Century.

Logan, J. and H. Molotch. 1987. *Urban Fortunes: The Political Economy of Place.* Berkeley: University of California Press.

Logue, J., R. Glass, W. Patton, A. Teodosio, and K. Thomas. 1998. *Participatory Employee Ownership—How It Works: Best Practices in Employee Ownership.* Pittsburgh: Worker Ownership Institute.

Lynd, S. 1997. *Living Inside Our Hope: A Steadfast Radical's Thoughts on Rebuilding the Movement.* Ithaca, NY: ILR Press.

Mann, M. 1986. *The Sources of Social Power.* vol. 1. Cambridge, UK: Cambridge University Press.

Martin, R. and B. Rowthorn (eds.). 1986. *The Geography of De-industrialization.* London: Macmillan.

Martinez, E. 2000. Where was the color in Seattle?: Looking for reasons why the Great Battle was so white. *Colorlines* 3: 1.

Massey, D. 1984. *Spatial Divisions of Labor.* New York: Routledge.

———. 1994. *Space, Place and Gender.* Minneapolis: University of Minnesota Press.

Matloff, Judith. 2002. Money hits: Stemming an epidemic of co-op crashes. *City Limits,* June.

McClaughry, J. 1969. Black Ownership and National Politics. In W. F. Haddah and G. D. Pugh (eds.). *Black Economic Development.* Englewood Cliffs, NJ: Prentice Hall.

McKee, B. 1995. South Bronx architecture. *The AIA Journal* 84(4): 86–95.
McKersie, R. B. 1968. Vitalize black enterprise. *Harvard Business Review*, September–October: 88–99.
McKnight, J. 1995. *The Careless Society: Community and Its Counterfeits.* New York: Basic Books.
Meek, C., W. Woodworth, and W. Dyer. 1988. *Managing By the Numbers: Absentee Ownership and the Decline of American Industry.* Reading, MA: Addison-Wesley.
Megson, J. and M. O'Toole. 1993. *Employee Ownership: The Vehicle for Community Development and Local Economic Control.* Boston: The Industrial Cooperatives Association.
Mele, C. 2000. *Selling the Lower East Side.* Minneapolis: University of Minnesota Press.
Mitchell, J. 1999. *Business Improvement Districts and Innovative Service Delivery.* The PricewaterhouseCoopers Endowment for the Business of Government.
Mitchell, R. and N. Shafter. 1984. *Standard Catalog of Depression Scrip of the United States.* Iola, WI: Kraus Publications.
Mittelbach, M. 1993. Downtown Bronx, USA. *City Limits*, March: 18–21.
Moody, K. 1997. *Workers in a Lean World.* London: Verso.
Munnell, A., G. Tootell, L. Browne, and J. McEneaney. 1996. Mortgage lending in Boston: Interpreting HMDA data. *American Economic Review* 86(1): 25–53.
National Alliance for Fair Employment. 2002. Contingent Work and Globalization. http://www.fairjobs.org/resources/, accessed June 10, 2002.
National Community Capital Association. 1999. *Making Your Money Make a Difference: 1999 Annual Report.* Philadelphia.
——— n.d. *Community Development Financial Institutions: Bridges Between Capital and Communities in Need* Philadelphia.
National Federation of Community Development Credit Unions. 1998. *Frequently Asked Questions About Community Development Credit Unions (CDCUs).* Philadelphia.
———. 1999. *Community Development Credit Unions at a Glance.* New York.
———. n.d. *About Community Development Credit Unions.* New York.
National Law Center on Homelessness and Poverty. 1998. *Homelessness and Poverty in America.* Washington, D.C.
National Low Income Housing Coalition. 1998. *1998 Advocate's Resource Book.* Washington, D.C.
Offe, C. and R. Heinze. 1992. *Beyond Employment: Time, Work and the Informal Economy* Alan Braley (trans.). Cambridge: Polity Press.
Olson, D. G. 1986–7. Employee ownership: An economic development tool for anchoring capital in local communities. *New York University Review of Law and Social Change* 15(1): 239–267.
Pacenza, M. 2002. Shaky Credit. *City Limits*, November.
Pacione, M. 1997. Local exchange trading systems as a response to the globalisation of capitalism. *Urban Studies* 34(8): 1179–1199.
———. 1999. The other side of the coin: local currency as a response to the globalization of capital, *Regional Studies* 33: 63–72.
Parzen, J. and M. Kieschnick. 1992. *Credit Where It's Due: Development Banking for Communities.* Philadelphia: Temple University Press.
Pateman, Carole. 1970. *Participation and Democratic Theory.* Cambridge: Cambridge University Press.
Perry, S. 1971. A note on the genesis of the Community Development Corporation. In C. G. Benello and D. Roussopoulos (eds.). *The Case For Participatory Democracy: Some Prospects for a Radical Society.* New York: Grossman Publishers.
———. 1972. Black institutions, Black separatism, and ghetto economic development. *Human Organization* 31(3): 1972.
Peterson, P. 1981. *City Limits.* Chicago: University of Chicago Press.
———. 1995. *State Responses to Welfare Reform: A Race to the Bottom?.* Washington, D.C.: The Urban Institute.
Peterson, Paul and Mark Rom. 1990. *Welfare Magnets: A New Case for a National Standard.* Washington, D.C.: Brookings Institute.
Pierce, N. and C. Steinbach. 1987. *Corrective Capitalism: The Rise of America's Community Development Corporations.* New York: Ford Foundation.
Piore, M. and C. Sabel. 1984. *The Second Industrial Divide: Possibilities for Prosperity.* New York: Basic Books.
Piven, F. F. and R. Cloward. 1977. *Poor People's Movements: Why They Succeed, How They Fail.* New York: Pantheon Books.

Planning. 1996. Presidential Award: South Bronx Comprehensive Community Revitalization Program 62(4): 6.

PolicyLink. 2002. *Equitable Development Toolkit.* Oakland, CA: Available online at: http://www.policylink.org/EquitableDevelopment/.

Porter, M. 1990. *The Competitive Advantage of Nations.* New York: Macmillan.

———. 1995. The competitive advantage of the inner city. *Harvard Business Review* 73 (May/June): 55–71.

———. 1997. New Strategies for Inner-City Economic Development. *Economic Development Quarterly* 11(1): 11–27.

Poulantzas, N. 1978. *State, Power, Socialism.* London: Verso.

Putnam, Robert. 1995. Bowling alone: America's declining social capital. *Journal of Democracy* 6:65–78.

———. 1996. The strange disappearance of civic America. *The American Prospect*, winter: 34–48.

———. 2000. *Bowling Alone.* New York: Simon and Schuster.

Queer Economic Justice Network. 2002. Welfare queens redefined: The search for 450 billion dollars. Paper presented at the Annual Creating Change Conference. November.

Rae, R. 1997. *Ownership and Equity: Perceptions of Home Ownership by Low Income Owners of Limited Equity Cooperative Housing.* Ph.D. dissertation, Graduate Faculty of Psychology, City University of New York.

Raines, J. C., L. E. Berson, and D. Gracie (eds.). 1982. *Community and Capital in Conflict: Plant Closings and Job Loss.* Philadelphia: Temple University Press.

Reich, R. 1991. *The Work of Nations.* New York: Alfred Knopf.

Repo, M. 1977. The fallacy of 'community control. In J. Cowley, A. Kaye, M. Mayo, and M. Thompson (eds.) *Community or Class Struggle?* London: Stage 1.

Ricker, Tom. 1998. *Estimating the Capital Costs of Community Destabilization: A Preliminary Report.* Washington, D.C.: National Center for Economic and Security Alternatives.

Robinson, C.F., A. Gilson. 1993. *Credit and the War on Poverty: An Analysis of the Credit Union Programs of the Office of Economic Opportunity.* Chicago: Woodstock Institute.

Roosevelt, F. and D. Belkin (eds.). 1994. *Why Market Socialism?* New York: M. E. Sharpe.

Rosenthal, C. 1994. Credit unions throw a lifeline to the poor. *New York Times,* 17 October.

Rowthorn, R. and R. Ramaswamy. 1997. *Deindustrialization: Causes and Implications.* IMF Working Paper 97/42. Washington, D.C.: International Monetary Fund.

Sass, R. J. and G. Stankiewicz, 2000. The Los Angeles Community Development Bank: The possible pitfalls of public-private partnerships. *Journal of Urban Affairs* 23(2): 133–155.

Sassen, S. 1991. *The Global City: New York, London, Tokyo.* Princeton, NJ: Princeton University Press.

———. 1998. *Globalization and Its Discontents.* New York: The New Press.

———. 2001. Emerging city as a space for new modalities of citizen life. Paper presented at the meeting of the International Sociological Association Research Committee on Regional and Urban Development. Amsterdam. 15 June.

Saunders, P. 1979. *Urban Politics.* London: Hutchinson.

Scanlon, William. 2001. *Nursing Workforce: Recruitment and Retention of Nurses and Nurse Aides Is a Growing Concern.* Government Accounting Office Testimony. May 17: 21.

Schill, M. 1999. *Housing and Community Development in New York City: Facing the Future.* Albany: State University of New York Press.

Schwartz, A. 1998. From confrontation to collaboration?: Banks, community groups, and the implementation of community reinvestment agreements. *Housing Policy Debate* 9(3): 631–662.

Sennett, R. 1977. *The Fall of Public Man.* New York: Alfred A Knopf.

Shapiro, I., R. Greenstein, and W. Primus. 2001. *Pathbreaking CBO Study Shows Dramatic Increases in Income Disparities in 1980s and 1990s: An Analysis of the CBO Data.* Washington, D.C.: Center on Budget and Policy Priorities.

Shavelson, J. 1990. *A Third Way: Innovations in Community-Owned Enterprise.* Washington, D.C.: The National Center for Economic Alternatives.

Shipp, Sigmund. 1996. The road not taken: Alternative strategies for Black economic development in the United States. *Journal of Economic Issues* 30(1): 79–95.

Shlay, A. 1999. Influencing the agents of urban structure: Evaluating the effects of community reinvestment organizing on bank lending practices. *Urban Affairs Review* 35(2): 247–278.

Shragge, E. and R. Fisher. 2001. Community development practices: New forms of regulation and/or potential for social change. Paper presented at the annual meeting of the Urban Affairs Association. Detroit. April.

Shuman, M. 1998. *Going Local: Creating Self-reliant Communities in a Global Age.* New York: Free Press.

Siegler, R. and H. Levy. n.d. *Brief History of Cooperative Housing.* Washington: National Association of Housing Cooperatives.

Sites, William. 1998. Communitarian theory and community development in the United States. *Community Development Journal* 33(1): 57–65.

Smith, N. 1979. Towards a Theory of Gentrification. *Journal of the American Planning Association* 45: 538–548.

———. 1993. Homeless/global: scaling places. In J. Bird, B. Curtis, T. Putnam, G. Robertson, and L. Tickner (eds.). *Mapping the Futures: Local Cultures, Global Change,* 87–119. New York: Routledge.

———. 1996. *The New Urban Frontier: Gentrification and the Revanchist City.* New York: Routledge.

Smith, N. and P. Williams (eds.). 1986. *Gentrification of the City.* Boston: Allen and Unwin.

Social Policy. 1979. Organizing Neighborhoods: Special Issue. September/October.

Spangenberg, E. 1998. President's remarks. Presentation at the Annual Meeting of the Bethex Federal Credit Union. Bronx, NY. October.

———. 1999. President, Bethex Federal Credit Union. Personal interview. May.

Squires, G. (ed.). 1992. *From Redlining to Reinvestment: Community Responses to Urban Disinvestment.* Philadelphia: Temple University Press.

Stein, A. 1986. Between Organization and Movement: ACORN and the Alinsky Model of Community Organizing. *Berkeley Journal of Sociology* 31: 93–115.

Stoecker, R. 1997. The CDC Model of Urban Redevelopment. *Journal of Urban Affairs* 19(1): 1–22.

Stone, M. 1993. *Shelter Poverty.* Philadelphia: Temple University Press.

Storper, M. 1997. *The Regional World.* New York: Guilford.

Sturdivant, F. D. 1969. The Limits of Black Capitalism. *Harvard Business Review.* January–February: 122–128.

———. 1971. Community Development Corporations: The Problem of Mixed Objectives. *Law and Contemporary Problems* 36: 35–50.

Tansey, C. 2001. Community Development Credit Unions: An Emerging Player in Low Income Communities. *Capital Xchange.* Washington, D.C.: Brookings Institute.

Taub, R. 1990. *Nuance and meaning in community development: Finding community and development.* New York: Community Development Research Center/New School for Social Research.

Taylor, P. 1982. A materialist framework for political geography. *Transactions of the Institute of British Geographers* 7: 15–34.

Tholin, K. 1994. *Community Development Financial Institutions: Investing in People and Communities.* Chicago: Woodstock Institute.

Tiebout, C. 1956. A pure theory of local expenditures. *Journal of Political Economy* 64: 416–424.

U.S. Department of Housing and Urban Development. 2000. *Rental Housing Assistance, The Worsening Crisis.* Washington, D.C.

Vidal, A. 1992. *Rebuilding communities: A National Study of Urban Community Development Corporations.* New York: Community Development Research Center/New School for Social Research.

———. 1996. CDCs as Agents of Neighborhood Change: The State of the Art. In D. Keating, et al. (eds.). *Revitalizing Urban Neighborhoods.* Lawrence: University of Kansas Press.

———. 1997. Can Community Development Re-Invent Itself? *Journal of the American Planning Association,* autumn: 429–438.

Walton, J. and D. Seddon. 1994. *Free Markets and Food Riots: The Politics of Global Adjustment.* Cambridge, MA: Blackwell.

Watkins, N. and K. Danaher. 2001. Boycotting World Bank bonds. In K. Danaher (ed.). *Democratizing the Global Economy.* Monroe, ME: Common Courage Press.

Weinberg, R. 1984. The use of eminent domain to prevent an industrial plant shutdown: The next step in an expanding power. *Albany Law Review* 49(1): 95–130.

Wilkenson, P. and J. Quarter. 1996. *Building a Community-Controlled Economy.* Toronto: University of Toronto Press.

Williams, M. 1997. *Credit to the Community: The Role of CDCUs in Community Development.* Chicago: Woodstock Institute.

————. 1998. *On the Move: An Analysis of Low-Income Credit Unions, 1990–1996*. Chicago: Woodstock Institute.

Williamson, J. 2002. Every Little Thing Counts. *The Guardian*, 2 May.

Williamson, T., D. Imbroscio, and G. Alperovitz. Forthcoming. *Place, Community and Democracy: Towards a Comprehensive Political Economic Framework for Renewing the Community Basis of Democracy in the Era of Globalization*. New York: Routledge.

Wills, J. 1998. A stake in place?: The geography of employee ownership and its implications for a stakeholding society. *Transactions of the Institute of British Geographers* 23: 79–94.

Wilson, J. Q. 1968. The urban unease: community vs. city. *The Public Interest* 12 (summer): 25–40.

Wilson, P. 1995. Embracing locality in local economic development. *Urban Studies* 32(4–5): 645–658.

Wolch, J. 1990. *The Shadow State: Government and Voluntary Sector in Transition*. New York: The Foundation Center.

Wolff, E. 2000. *Recent Trends in Wealth Ownership, 1983–1998*. Annandale, NY: Jerome Levy Economics Institute.

Wolman, H. with D. Sptizley. 1999. The politics of local economic development. In John Blair and Laura Reese (eds.) *Approaches to Economic Development*. Thousand Oaks, CA: Sage.

Worth, R. 1999. Guess who saved the South Bronx?: Big government. *Washington Monthly*, April: 26–33.

Young, H 1988. The long running premier. *The Guardian*. 2 January.

Zdenek, R. 1987. Community Development Corporations. In S. Bruyn and J. Meehan (eds.). *Beyond the Market and the State: New Directions in Community Development*. Philadelphia: Temple University Press.

Index